I DIDN'T KNO ... CK

GROWING UP BLACK IN THE WHITE WORLD OF TENNIS

A MEMOIR BY
STEVEN-PIERRE RYUSE

WITH FRANCIE J. NOLAN

DEDICATION

In memory of my brother, Mark Ryuse, Jr.
whose life was much too short
but had a lasting impact on my life
and the lives of many others

CONTENTS

FOREWORD

I didn't think I was nervous as I entered Olympic Indoor Tennis Club at the age of 16. I'd been in tennis clinics my whole life, and I knew the kids in this clinic and certainly wasn't nervous about not being able to keep up with them. Still, for some reason the butterflies had made their way into my stomach as I entered "The Bubble" that day.

I was joining a new program with a new pro; one whom I'd had brief interactions with growing up in the tennis world, one who wore a Big Ten Championship ring on his finger and a handkerchief around his neck. One who, in many ways, was the antithesis of all the previous tennis pros to whom I had been exposed. Not only was his skin tone darker than the pros I was used to working with, but also his personality was different from the intensity so many pros or coaches employ. He was confident and "laid back" as an instructor and a competitor. Everything he did looked effortless, from simply feeding balls to his students to his point play with the better kids. While other pros scurried and scampered to hit big shots followed by big yells to impress their students, this guy didn't do any of that. If the ball was out of reach, he'd glide across the court as if it were made of ice, timing it so that his last step provided him the momentum to rip a devastating forehand that left opponents and spectators in awe. He didn't subscribe to the plain, boring outfits that stereotype the tennis fashion industry. He wore colors. Bright blues and shining purples, always matching, always cool.

My first real interaction with Steven Ryuse came about halfway through that first clinic. I wasn't nervous about my tennis game or how Steven would be impressed with my skills on the court; I was more nervous about what Steven would think of me as a person. At the time, and during my whole childhood, I grew up in the wealthiest suburb in Columbus, Upper Arlington (even though there's no Lower Arlington, the founders needed the Upper to feel good). "UA" as it is called in shorthand, was one of the last suburbs in Columbus, Ohio, to allow people of color to own property. I could count my black classmates on one finger and my black teachers on one hand. Did Steven know UA's history? Would he hold me accountable? Ridiculous thoughts like this made their way into my head as I made my way to Steven's court.

"Who's that on your shirt?" he asked me, without saying hello or asking how I liked his clinic.

"Jimi Hendrix" I answered nervously, looking down to see what tee-shirt was at the top of my drawer that day. Like most teenagers, I was way too cool to care about what shirt I was wearing. If it was on top, I grabbed it.

"You can't hear Jimi!" he yelled across the net at me.

Luckily for me, I'd seen the movie *White Men Can't Jump* and knew that part of the movie pretty well, or perhaps that comment would've put me on the defensive. Instead, it became an inside joke between the two of us for the rest of that clinic and for clinics to come. I'd wear my Jimmy Buffet shirt, point to it, and yell "You can't hear this Jimmy!" and we'd both laugh at the absurd contrast between the music of Hendrix and Buffet.

To be honest, I don't remember too much else about Steven's drills. I know I finished the three-month clinic, played my high-school season, and never went back. It's funny how things work out, though. That was just the beginning of my relationship with Steven Ryuse.

Ten years later, I found myself working that very clinic that I had participated in as a youth. Steven was now my boss even though he treated me as an equal and as a friend. We worked in the winter season at Olympic and both of us had country club jobs that kept us busy in the summer. During the late winter of 2008, Steven came up to me at Olympic Tennis Club.

"I need to talk to you," he said.

"What's up, man? Is everything all right?" I asked, since he never started a conversation that way.

"I need a job this summer. Just found out they're screwing me over at my club. You got one for me?" There was no self pity, no sorrow, not even discouragement in his voice. He came asking a former student of his for a job, like he was asking for a ride down the street.

"You got it!" I replied, not sure how I'd make it work, but I knew I would.

The past three summers, Steven and I have worked together, spending eight to twelve hours a day at the same workplace for months at a time. As a wide-eyed sixteen-year-old, I thought he made teaching indoors look easy. I still have no idea how he makes it through the summer. While the rest of us make sure not to schedule back-to-back lessons when it's scorching hot outside, Steven teaches six to eight hours at a time, stopping in the air conditioning every so often to make sure he doesn't break a sweat!

During our times together, I've had the privilege of learning about not just tennis, but life, from Steven Ryuse. Throughout the election of Barack Obama,

America's first black president, I never once heard Steven comment on someone else's race or ethnicity as a way of describing someone or in referring to a person's behavior. Race is something Steven doesn't usually comment on, and it's something I've never really heard him discuss in all the years I've known him. By reading his book we get some insight as to what has shaped Steven's views and what it's been like for a black man growing up in a white town, competing in a white man's sport.

My first encounter with Steven taught me the most valuable lesson *I Didn't Know I Was Black* has to offer: that my insecurities that day were there because of how I saw things as a white kid, nervous to meet my black tennis instructor. Steven, on the other hand, didn't see any of that. He didn't see me as a spoiled white kid from a mainly white suburb. Instead, he saw me as he wanted to be seen: as a tennis player, a competitor, and a person. His "color blindness," in my case, has been contagious.

Amos Allison
Head Pro
Worthington Hills Country Club
Worthington, Ohio

FOREWORD

As a young boy, Steven began playing tennis with his father and brother at Columbus, Ohio's Beatty Park and Wolfe Park tennis courts in the late 1960s. Wolfe Park public courts were highly popular, having six courts with night- play lighting.

Players came from all over. The surrounding areas from where they came included the Columbus suburbs of Bexley and Whitehall, as well as outlying areas as far away as Mount Vernon. All devoted public court players would meet at Beatty Park and Wolfe Park because they liked the variety of quality and levels of the tennis players there.

Older and more seasoned players were many. Some notable players come to mind. Just to mention a few, I remember Stan Dixon, Bill Hairston, Jim Spivey, Lee Townsel, John Thomas, Bob Morton, and Jim Criswell. Jim is now the manager of Olympic Tennis Club.

Steven arrived on the scene about the same time as John Gurian, a top "juniors" player. That was their age bracket. They later became teammates on The Ohio State University men's tennis team. Steven soon became a challenge to all of us because of his great desire to compete. I remember that he would actually dive after a ball that was out of reach. And — THESE WERE HARD COURTS!

Presently, Steven is a most respected tennis professional at Olympic Tennis Club. He continues to be in demand by up and coming youngsters as well as adults.

Frank Barnett,
Former U.S. National Ranking #11
55 and over Singles Category
Ranked #1 Midwest Senior Category

ACKNOWLEDGEMENTS

I would like to express deep gratitude for those early relatives who paved the way for me to grow up in a simple, peaceful village in central Ohio. Likewise, I am grateful for my mother and father who were my first and most important tennis instructors; and my sisters who have encouraged me along the journey.

A special recognition goes to Nancy McFarland and Linda Augspurger who were first to believe in this project. This book would not have been possible without their help and the editorial assistance of Michael Minutilli. I also would like to acknowledge others who have helped with this book: Denise Green, Kathy Starks, Dane Shavers, and Miles Harris.

INTRODUCTION

My intent in writing this book is to share my experiences as a black man growing up in a predominantly white society. As I reflect on my life, I find that tennis has permeated all aspects of it. It seems to be infused into my very being. For me tennis and life are almost one and the same. Tennis is, in many ways, a parable of life. Because of the strong feelings I have for tennis, I have selected a tennis tip with which to begin each chapter. The tip will connect the sport to my experiences in life. I will look at both hardship and success through a lens of tennis precepts.

The book describes my journey in two worlds: the black world of my family and the white world of tennis in which I have spent the greatest part of my life. Having a strong sense of self and developing pride in your heritage are valuable elements of growing up. A strong foundation enables us to withstand fault lines, storms, and other damages that come our way.   Race may be determined by biology; however, identity emerges from interaction in society. It is only when we accept ourselves as we are, that we are able to reach out to others and accept them.

I have tried to create an honest account of my life and the positive impact of tennis. Tennis is a game; we know that life is more than a game. However, when we adopt some of the rules of tennis to our daily lives, we can come out on the winning side.

Certain names have been changed in an effort to protect the privacy of individuals.

CHAPTER ONE

Tennis Tip: Volleying is really simple: all you want to do is punch the ball into the open court. The less you swing, the less your chance for error. The forehand volley is the one you miss most often because the racket has the tendency to get behind you. You want to keep the racket out front. When the racket gets behind you, you swing at the ball instead of punching the ball with the racket.

The May morning in 1965 was warm and balmy as the school bus trudged along on the forty-minute trip to school. I was nine years old, and trying to sort out my place in the world. The long bus ride to Amity Elementary School from our home in Mount Vernon gave me time to think about things. I couldn't understand, as we bounced along over country roads, why we had to make this long bus ride when there was an elementary school located only a few blocks from our house. Mom told us it was because Amity didn't have any black kids, and we were sent out to "integrate" Amity's school. I didn't know what that word meant, but I knew it was strange and uncomfortable for me, and I didn't quite understand the part about being selected to ride the bus because we lived on the northern side of town.

I sat several rows back from my brother, Mark, who was a fifth-grader, two years and two grades ahead of me. I had my James Bond 007 lunch box by my side. In our small town of Mount Vernon, Ohio, we belonged to one of the few – less than one percent – black families that comprised the population of 13,073. My family's roots were deep in Mount Vernon's soil. My great-great-uncle, Joseph Booker (on my mother's side), was freed from slavery when he was ten. He was one of seven children sired by their slave owner. His mother, Sarah, had traveled in a horse and wagon from the plantation in Beverly, Virginia (now West Virginia), across the Ohio River into Martin's Ferry and then to Barnesville.

Steven is in the middle row, second from left

They settled in a Quaker settlement in Barnesville. As the children grew up there, beginning in the late 1800s, some of them headed north to Mount Vernon because of employment opportunities. Joseph found a job as caretaker to one of the Cooper Brothers who established the Cooper Bessemer Corporation, later known as Cooper Energy Services where my mother would eventually hold a job. Through family stories passed down by my mother and grandmother, I knew that our ancestors had been productive and accepted members in Mount Vernon. I was proud of their contributions to the community's arts and other organizations that are vital to a growing community.

Like most American families, my family's ancestry was varied. Intermingling of blacks and whites was an outcome of slavery. Thomas Jefferson's black offspring, for example, which diluted the black race in varying degrees, resulted in a multiethnic status all under the umbrella of "black." I've been told that on my father's side there is Cherokee; on my mother's side, a Jewish great- grandfather. My great-grandmother passed down a light complexion and green eyes to my brother and me. My sister Valerie inherited hazel eyes; and sister Kiersten, brown eyes. Perhaps because of our light skin color and the color of our eyes, we felt more similar, than different, from our friends in Mount Vernon. We were just another family in a rural small town in Ohio.

My mother's life as a young girl growing up in Mount Vernon resembled my childhood as she grew up in the same part of this small town. During lazy summers I played "hide-and-seek" with friends and operated Kool-Aid stands for a little pocket change. Mom told me she had sold corn-on-the-cob, along with popsicles made from Kool-Aid, to wash down the corn. I imagined Mom in pig tails yelling "Corn for sale!" The thought made me grin. Little Dian Hammond was well known around Mount Vernon as the kid who established a library. Mom had a collection of comic books which she developed into a lending library. She glued cards into each comic book and kept track of which neighborhood kid had borrowed a particular comic book. I never knew how steep the "late" fines were, but admired Mom's hustle and bustle.

Mom's parents had a nice, large home in the northern part of town, and her mother was well respected as a pianist who played at the Methodist and Baptist churches in Mount Vernon. Grandmother gave piano lessons to kids both black and white. Grandmother also had a day job as a maid for local hotels. Mom told us a comical story of how she would confuse the ushers at the local movie house. The Vine Theater was segregated; the left side was reserved for blacks and the right side for whites. Mom would always sit on the left side at least for a little while. When the ushers noticed Mom, who was so light in color, they told her to move to the right side where the white folks sat. She was "acting white" (but not because she wanted to) long before the expression came into being. I thought that would be a funny trick to play because of the custom of segregating the theater.

Mom's family lived primarily among whites with relative tranquility. But my grandmother, I learned, had a stubborn streak. For instance, if the Methodists wouldn't serve her communion for some reason, she would abandon them and go play piano for the Baptists, and vice versa. I heard also from Mom that Grandmother didn't like flamboyant preachers. No one was able to pull the wool over her eyes. She didn't put up with much, and I liked that about her.

My dad, on the other hand, did not have such a peaceful childhood. He grew up in Mansfield (Ohio), the county seat of Richland County and over three times the size of Mount Vernon with a much larger black population. While Mom may have experienced a "hushed" form of discrimination, available in most northern small towns, Dad got the overt brand, which included racial slurs, on a regular basis. He was dark-skinned and had to be careful to not over-step his bounds. Because of the racial pain he endured growing up in Mansfield, he had a difficult time relating to whites at the time he met my mother. When I asked him once how he had managed to grow up without getting seriously hurt in fights, being shot, or turning to criminal behavior, he told me that it was because he always thought ahead. He continued by saying that he tried to always go out with a group rather than alone because there was safety in groups. The black population today in Mansfield is around 20%, and in Mount Vernon it is still only 1%, significantly below the state average.

My dad's family had migrated in the early 1900s from Tennessee to settle in Mansfield and work in the steel mill. Even though the work was back-breaking, it paid better than any jobs they had held previously. When my father completed high school in Mansfield, he joined the navy where he received an injury from shrapnel in an explosion on an ammunition barge. After receiving an honorable discharge, he returned to Mansfield and married a local woman. The marriage turned out to be a disaster as his bride left him for another man after running up substantial debt for Dad to pay. A divorce was granted shortly after she skipped town. Not long after that, Dad met Mom.

The story goes that Dad, a "high style Romeo," dressed in the Cab Calloway/Duke Ellington fashion of that period – side-brim fedora, peg pants, key chains hanging – quickly captured Mom's attention when he and his buddies rolled into Mount Vernon on "Black Night" at the skating rink. Dad and his friends would travel regularly to neighboring towns (e.g. Delaware, Marion, Zanesville, Columbus, Newark, and Mount Vernon) for the pleasure of dancing, skating, socializing, and scoping out the pretty young women. Mount Vernon became Dad's last stop on the line after he met Mom. He was smitten right away by her moves on the skating rink; and, later, on the dance floor.

This is a photo of Dian (Mom) skating

Roller skating and dances, the two big social attractions of that era, were segregated. Blacks were allowed at the rinks and dance clubs on only one specific night each week. It is curious that no one protested the unfairness of the rule. They became accustomed to it and accepted it. If blacks wanted to skate more often than once a week, thus having a wider range of social activity, they had to have access to a set of wheels. For that reason they traveled by carload to the neighboring towns that scheduled "black night" on various days of the week. It wasn't long before Mom and Dad were going to roller rinks and dances all around the area. Buckeye Lake, which wasn't too far east of Columbus, had an amusement park. They liked going there and riding the roller coaster and Ferris wheel. However, it was also segregated with only one night a week allotted to blacks.

I remember being told that, as their relationship developed, Mom introduced Dad to tennis. At that time tennis was an elite sport played mostly at private county clubs, not public parks. Since blacks couldn't join country clubs, access to tennis was limited for them. However, Mom had no problem playing tennis at Riverside, the public park near her home, since she was light-skinned and didn't stand out. She quickly learned the game and would spend all day, day after day at Riverside Park and find "pick-up" games. She was determined and eager to play as much as possible and improve. She'd go to the park early with a sack lunch and a jug of Kool-Aid to last her all day. In the evening she would often return to the park and keep on playing. She remembers that one day, when she was 16 years old, she played three matches of singles starting at 1 PM and going until 7 PM. She won all three.

After she met Dad, she infected him with her tennis bug and helped him improve his game. My dad had played a little tennis at night in Mansfield since blacks were not allowed on the courts during daylight hours. With Mom's help, he soon became an outstanding player as a result of natural talent, perseverance, and love of the game. During their courtship and after they were married, Mom and Dad would spend every day they could playing tennis.

This is a photo of the wedding of Mark, Sr., and Dian

As summer vacation was only a month away, I was looking forward to playing "cops and robbers" in the woods with my friends and building rafts out of inner tubes and other items we found around the creek bank. I was also thinking about adding corn-on-the-cob to my Kool-Aid stand as Mom had. As I sat on the bus thinking about my family and imagining what life had been like for Mom and Dad when they were my age, I wasn't thinking about playing tennis myself. Even though I had watched my parents play lots of games, I had not tried it. When they played, Mark, my sisters and I played on the swings and other things at the park. I did enjoy playing tetherball and other games on the playground at school and looked forward to recess and physical education class since I had a problem sitting for long stretches doing work sheets or reading. I was not a good reader and I learned better when I could get my body involved instead of just my brain.

Across the aisle from me and three seats back on the bus sat Valerie, my little sister who was in first grade. She was chatting quietly with a little friend. I heard her mention Kiersten, our baby sister who was just a toddler and spent her days with a babysitter while Mom worked as a secretary. At home I would notice Valerie playing "school" with Kiersten as her student. Kiersten was learning from Valerie as I learned from Mark. In our family, and probably with others of a similar make up, the girls stuck together and so did the boys. Of course, if any one of us was in trouble, we all were there to stick up for each other.

It seemed on that spring morning, as I was reflecting on my way to school, that my family was no different than any other in Mount Vernon. We worked, played, fussed, went to church, laughed and cried together. As the bus moved along toward school, I felt comfortable sitting by myself far behind my brother and his buddies. Rarely would I willingly go near them, because Mark liked to tease me. Instead of calling me Steven, he would refer to me as "Chunky." I was sure that he chose the name to remind me of my chubbiness and my need to be more active in sports as he was. I hated to be called Chunky, and despised my brother when he would come out with it in front of others. So, I stayed far enough behind him to avoid being noticed and addressed as Chunky but remained in hearing distance.

The windows of the bus were open to the morning air, and I became aware of sweet smells that came from the blooming trees and bushes along the road. I was thinking about the kickball game that was scheduled for my class in the afternoon and smiled to myself as I imagined the chance to show off my athletic abilities.

I may be chunky, I thought, but I know how to kick a ball, and I'm a fast runner. I'll show my brother and his friends. I was feeling confident as the bus finally turned the corner with the view of school up ahead.

The warm morning air in the countryside can hold an assortment of smells. As the bus slowed to a stop, I was jolted out of my day-dreaming by the disgusting odor of skunk. I held my breath as I got off the bus as fast as I could and hurried into the building. I wanted to escape the foul odor and also hoped that it wouldn't stick to me.

I soon settled into a typical school day as morning crept into afternoon. After lunch we were lined up to go out onto the playground for the kickball game. I started off playing well, just as I had imagined on my trip to school. I guess you could say that I was playing above my head. It was paying off too. The score was tied in the final inning with 2 outs, and I was up to kick. The outcome of the game depended on me. I connected with the ball, and it traveled way back to hit the fence at the end of the field. I dashed from base to base and came in to score the winning point. I was panting for breath when I heard a voice shouting.

"You're a nigger!" The words exploded into the warm sunshine of that spring afternoon. As I looked up from home plate, I saw Floyd, who had pitched the ball.

His face was red, and his fists were clenched. I realized that his angry stare was directed at me.

He yelled it again, just in case I had missed it the first time, adding, "My dad says you are a nigger, too!"

My emotions were conflicted. I was thrilled to have scored the winning run in the kickball game. I had never done that before, and it felt good. Winning points in a tight game like that is the currency of youth. That feeling of pride, however, lasted only briefly as my mind registered on the ugly word that had spewed from Floyd's mouth. I knew that word from history, and realized that it wasn't a good one to be called. Why would Floyd call me that? After my brief analysis of his outburst, I reacted reflexively by walking over to where he stood and punching him in his red face. Hard! He fell backward, and his nose began to bleed.

I had been called names before, mostly by my brother. I didn't like it, but it seemed to come with the territory of being a younger brother to him. Being called nigger, though, struck a nerve with me because it was based on the color of my skin and my heritage. This was not only a personal attack on me; but also an insult to my family and my life.

In that brief episode, on a small rural schoolyard in Amity, Ohio, I crossed a line from which I could never return. I had never thought of myself as different until then. I had never distinguished between blacks and whites, and no one had asked me to. Until that afternoon I had felt accepted in school where I was surrounded by whites; and, equally accepted at home with my black family. Now, in one blast of anger, my place in the world shifted. Suddenly I was made to realize that I was part of two distinct worlds: a white one and a black one. The knowledge hit me in my gut. I realized that I was different (black) even though my outward appearance had not changed. My skin was still light and my eyes still green, but that didn't matter. I now knew that skin color made a difference to some people, and had the power to enrage others. This knowledge was going to change my life.

The teacher quickly separated us and announced to the class that they needed to line up and wait for her. She was taking us to the office for the principal to handle this. My classmates were unusually quiet as Floyd and I went with Ms. Jones into the principal's office. Floyd was holding a blood-soaked cloth to his nose, and I guess it was obvious from Ms. Jones' exasperation and the look on my face as she yanked me forward that I was responsible for the blood. The principal accurately assessed the situation; and, with her arms crossed, looked down at me and admonished: "Steven, I'm surprised. You've never been in trouble before. Why did you do this to Floyd?"

I lowered my head, unsure of how to respond. The teacher spoke for both Floyd and me by recounting exactly what had taken place. The principal did then what most principals do: she called the parents.

As I sat squirming in the large, wooden chair with my legs dangling and my arms hanging loosely at my sides, I began to wonder how my father would have handled the incident on the playground. My dad had shared with me about the times he had felt the sting of discrimination and prejudice as he was growing up in Mansfield. Because of his harsh life experiences, his practice was to teach his children to accept everyone and look beyond skin color to the unique beauty within each person. Both of my parents had taught us to be mentally color blind. But, I wondered, in the heat of the moment, would Dad have punched a kid who had called him the "N" word? In my mind I was answering, "Yep!" I was brought back to the present by the words of Floyd's father who had entered the room, along with my mother.

Floyd's dad walked over and took the chair next to Floyd while Mom stood by me. I got up and gave her my chair. After hearing from the teacher about the kickball game and resultant name calling, Floyd's dad turned toward his son. "I think you should apologize to Steven. I can't imagine what got into you."

Floyd came over to me and extended his hand. With his voice barely above a whisper, he apologized. I then apologized to him for bloodying his nose. My mother and Floyd's dad nodded to one another and smiled as we left the principal's office. The principal seemed satisfied that justice has been done as she shifted some papers on her desk.

We were kids after all, and I think neither of us truly understood the implication of the word. Even though I felt that an apology from me was the appropriate response, I had no remorse for hitting him because I felt he deserved it. With that word he had completely and utterly offended me. We later became friends and the "N" word was never brought up again. It is amazing to me, however, how vividly I still remember that day in the third grade. That day was the first time in my life I felt different from other kids.

Just as punching the ball in volleying at the net is important; at times in life it becomes necessary to use a punch to make a point. You don't want the racket to get behind you when volleying; instead, it needs to stay out front. In order to put life's issues behind us and move forward, we need to bring them out front where we can deal with life directly and move forward after doing so. As a child, I punched; as an adult I look for more sophisticated options to make my point.

CHAPTER TWO

Tennis Tip: Don't come in unless you receive an invitation. You need to receive a short ball or make a very aggressive shot to come into the net from the baseline and be successful whether playing singles or doubles. If you come in just because you want to try to take the net, you'll find yourself losing more points than winning them because there's too much court on both sides of you to cover, and your opponent has more time to make a passing shot.

Because my dad had not only experienced a lot of prejudice growing up, but also had belonged to a family that struggled near the poverty line, he was tough. Life had hardened him in a beneficial way and molded his resolve to strive for more. He was determined to make a better life for his family, yet he retained some of the ideas of his father that made things difficult for his kids.

For instance, if one of us got into trouble, he punished all of us. Punishment meant using a belt.

After Dad met Mom and they decided later to marry, he was determined to get into a line of work that would provide well for his family. As a young man he had worked at a dry cleaners store and had other low-paying jobs with limited opportunities for better pay. He took advantage of the G.I. bill for his education. After rigorous assessment to determine specific aptitudes and skills, he learned that he was mechanically inclined and would do well at jobs where he could take things apart and fix them. After looking at various colleges, he enrolled at Bradley University in Peoria, Illinois. At that time, my parents sold their little house in Mount Vernon for extra cash for Dad's college and living expenses. They decided it would be best if Mom and two-year-old Mark moved into the house with Grandmother. Mom was already pregnant with me at the time, so living with Grandmother would be much easier for her as well as Mark and me.

I'm sure it was difficult for my parents to live apart, but they were willing to sacrifice for a brighter future for their kids. They visited back and forth regularly, and Dad was always just a phone call away when we needed him. He finished the program in three years during which time I was born. Then he came back to Mount

Vernon to open a watch repair shop and thought he was set for success. He had bought equipment from three local jewelers and made a heavy investment in a business whose years, unfortunately, were numbered. With the development of Timex watches, customers dwindled because, instead of paying for watch repairs, they disposed of broken watches and bought the cheaper new ones.

Seeking a new line of employment, with two kids and a wife to support, Dad had to re-assess his skills. He went to the nearby Aerospace Base in Heath, Ohio, just outside Newark. The skills he had acquired at Bradley made it possible for him to qualify for a program in precision repair of gyroscopes and accelerometers in inertial guidance systems. This required another upset for the family. This time the move was to Long Island, New York. Mom was pregnant with Valerie at the time, and the drive to see Dad required a 12-hour train ride. At the end of his training, he returned to Mount Vernon and purchased a new house for us. Valerie was born there in 1958.

During the early years of their marriage and later on, too, Dad learned through Mom to trust whites. He had never done that before because he had such bad memories of his growing-up years and blamed most of his bad fortune on prejudice. His new attitude of trust leveled, mellowed, and expanded him so that he joined the mainstream of America. He would no longer use prejudice and bias as an excuse not to succeed. Instead, he would find ways to work within the system and persevere in order to reach his goals.

In spite of this new outlook, Dad still carried a lot of the old baggage. For instance, he had been taught male dominance from his dad, precluding the idea that women could be equally ranked. That attitude caused friction and resulted in many disagreements between Mom and him. My mother was an independent, confident and competent woman who found she could wear many hats and keep several balls in the air simultaneously. She held her ground with Dad not only on race issues but also on the status of women. In spite of occasional arguments where she had to stand up for herself when he was being "macho," they could share laughter and good times through tennis. Tennis brought them together and provided an avenue of success for their children.

My mom had a well of optimism that I drew from as I grew up. She had never come head to head with any direct racism, the awful kinds of discrimination or prejudice that my dad had experienced. She explained to us that she had never looked for it and that "you can't expect to find racism hidden under rocks." With her having that outlook, when she faced adversity, prejudice was the very last place she looked when confronted with problems.

Her family, too, was completely different from my dad's. While my father had grown up in a one-room shanty, my mother's family had a ten-room house filled with nice furniture. Mom accepted her place in life and expected the best. She believed that there were no excuses for not performing and would never accept race as an excuse for failure. Then, too, a long line of professional people emanated from her family. Her Aunt Viola was the first African-American registered nurse in Knox County. As incredible as it sounds, mom's great-grandmother ran a beauty shop that catered to only white clientele. Mom always told us to think beyond the limits and expect to achieve.

In spite of that, we knew that racial overtones in small northern towns like Mt. Vernon did exist although they were subtle and didn't appear to be barriers. Like citizens of other small towns in the America of the mid 1960s, in Mount Vernon we were well insulated from urban unrest and civil rights issues that were boiling over at that time in the nation's history. I was just a small-town kid like every other kid in Mount Vernon. Other folks were simply my friends or my family. Since I grew up in a small country town, I found out later that

I had little in common with urban kids, white or black. My environment played a larger role in defining me than did my color. As it turned out, growing up in a "small white town" would serve me better in my later life than I ever could have imagined.

I had two good friends in my neighborhood who were black but they went to private, Catholic schools. That left me with only white schoolmates, but I did enjoy playing with Vincent and Charles after school, on weekends and in the summer. I remember the summer before I started junior high. Charles, Vincent and I built a boat using two inner tubes from tires with a crate in between them. We floated down the Kokosing River, which was a blast.

Sports had started to interest me in grade school. I became interested in tennis as the result of watching my parents play. As I watched them, I saw how much happiness they shared while playing tennis together. As we kids grew up, they played tennis at the park near our home for hours at a time while we played in sand boxes and on teeter-totters and swings. Since Mom and Dad were so excited over tennis, I guess it was natural that all four of their kids eventually would want to share in that joy. I remember from my earliest years that on a typical Saturday Mom would pack a picnic lunch and we'd be at the park all day. Mark and I watched out for our sisters as they played.

It was also interesting to hear them talk about tennis events of the day such as the "Battle of the Sexes" between Billie Jean King and Bobby Riggs and how that spectacle advanced tennis, especially for women and minorities, since Billie Jean won. Billie Jean King said about tennis: "Victory is fleeting, but losing is forever." Neither Mom nor Dad liked to lose, so they would play game after game until each was satisfied that he or she had given the best game they had. I didn't know much about Billie Jean King at the time or Bobby Riggs. When I asked about them, I was told that Bobby Riggs may have been the most underrated of all the top players, and he was 53 years old when he and Billie Jean played their famous match. Mom said that no one knows what would have happened if Billie Jean had lost that match. Her winning it, though, put women's tennis on the map.

Life continued for our family in much the same way as Mom's family before us in the quiet town. After sixth grade, I was able to return to Mount Vernon's junior high school and say good-by to Amity. Valerie and Kiersten were still attending and helping to "integrate" the country school. Valerie was in fourth grade, and Kiersten rode with her on the bus as a first grader. Valerie sometimes had to wake up Kiersten when she fell asleep on the long morning and afternoon rides each day. The summer before I was to attend junior high, Mark was bound for high school.

Leaving the limited curriculum of Amity behind, I found new opportunities in junior high in Mount Vernon. I especially liked being in the choir, and I remember being bold enough to do a solo, a song from a popular group called the Monkees. They were a popular Beatles-like rock quartet that formed in the late 1960s. The group produced many successful hits and a television show. *I'm a Believer* and *The Last Train to Clarksville* are two of their most popular hits. The humorous Monkees' song, *This Just Doesn't Seem to Be My Day,* was my choice to perform at school because I liked the lines and also liked making people laugh. I sang it at home with my imaginary guitar and discovered that I could hold an audience. The lyrics go something like this: "I guess I should have stayed in bed, a pillow wrapped around my head. My, oh my, oh my . . . how I wish she would have stayed . . . This just doesn't seem to be my day." Performing the song at a school concert was positive attention and altogether different from being "the class clown" in elementary school. It felt good to be appreciated for having musical talent as well as a sense of humor.

Like most kids, I was naive about life outside my hometown. I had no idea that black people were treated differently from whites in the south. The news media didn't emphasize the problems, leaving me unaware that there was a racial divide in the country. It was not until junior high school that I began to hear about the Civil Rights movement in the south even though the historic March on Washington, led by Dr. Martin Luther King, Jr., had occurred in August of 1963 when I was in the fourth grade. I quickly learned more about racism as I entered into the world of sports and my experiences widened. As it turned out, tennis, a sport played largely by whites, was to be the catalyst that made all the difference in my education and profession. Without the strong sense of acceptance of all cultures and positive expectation that my mother built into me, I may not have made tennis my career choice.

One of the top ten tennis players at the time was a black player, Arthur Ashe, who would go on to beat the number one player in the world, Jimmy Connors, in a match that was supposed to be a slaughter at Wimbledon in 1972. He was the first African American man to win there, and took tennis to a new level for the black community. He gave hope and encouragement to tennis playing families like mine. Arthur Ashe inspired others because of his moral courage, dignity and courtesy both on and off the tennis court. When his peers – John McEnroe and Jimmy Connors –

displayed loud, outlandish and disrespectful conduct during tennis matches, Ashe played with respect for his opponent, linesmen, and others. The contrast was glaring. If someone were to ask me who my role model has been, I would have to answer Arthur Ashe. I got to see him play at a local country club although it was highly unusual for a black man to play at a Columbus country club in the 1970s.

From 1974-77, Jimmy Connors was ranked the top player in the world. His antics on the court helped get the crowd involved and made tennis exciting, but not in a positive way. He could be rude and vulgar at times. Ashe criticized him for playing in lucrative tournaments and not playing for his country as a member of the Davis Cup team. Connors later sued Ashe for that. Connors' dislike of Ashe continued even after Ashe's death when he wouldn't attend the dedication of the Arthur Ashe Stadium at the U.S. Open.

The media referred to Connors as a Tennis Brat and John McEnroe, who could be even more outlandish in his disrespect for linesmen and umpires, as "Super Brat." In spite of that title, John McEnroe was probably one of the best tennis players of all time. I respect both champions who have used their fame and fortune to provide opportunities for under-privileged kids to learn tennis. John McEnroe has established many charities and foundations for at-risk and disadvantaged youth.

Most sports are easier learned when you're a child. Chris Evert, one of the tennis stars that all the guys had a crush on, started lessons when she was five years old. She was an American tennis champion by age 16. It was Tracy Austen, another superb young star, who broke Chrissie's record of winning 125 consecutive matches in 1979. My dad started teaching me tennis when I was twelve years old. Compared to the age when Dad learned tennis, twelve was young. However, compared to the kids I would be facing in tournaments later on, twelve was old to begin learning the game. I discovered later in my life at Ohio State that most of the kids on the team had received lessons from a pro when they were as young as six years old. Dad had been playing tennis with Mark, who was just finishing eighth grade, and I wanted to be a part of that special time they spent together.

After junior high school, Vincent, Charles and I began to drift farther apart as they became immersed in their school's activities and associated with a different set of friends. I was ready and eager to join Mark and Dad on the courts, realizing that tennis was the key to getting attention from Dad.

Mark had taken well to tennis from the start. Encouraged by Mark's quick progress, Dad got me a wooden racket and I joined them on the court at Riverside where they regularly played. Mark was already very good, and he agreed with Dad that I had a knack for the game. Eager to please my brother and my dad, I gave it my best, and it wasn't long before I was a captive of the sport. The more I played, the more I wanted to play.

Mom's tennis took a back seat as Dad started working with Mark and me. Not only was Mom very consumed with her family, but she was looking for a career change. She had worked for the Federal Housing Administration, completing home loan applications and interviewing prospective home buyers, but was looking for a more lucrative job at the time with Cooper Energy Services.

As a young girl, she had made a name for herself, however, in tennis around Mount Vernon. When she was in high school, she was petite; however, she could beat all the large, athletic girls. She played for five summers and was the Mount Vernon City Champion until Violet Vanderhorst took her down. Violet was 26, and Mom was 18. They didn't have junior's classification at the time; they put all the women in one category. Against Violet, Mom had not a chance. After Violet beat her so handily, she told me, she sat by the river and bawled. That scenario occurred during the summer of 1950.

Sometimes Mom would bring nine-year-old Valerie and six-year-old Kiersten, to watch Mark and me play tennis with Dad in late afternoons, Saturdays, and in the summer. Mom would show the girls how to bounce balls using her racket, but they were usually more interested in playing in the sand or with their dolls at that time. I would notice at times, though, that Valerie, even at the age of nine, seemed to be getting into the game a little bit when she would clap when I won a point from Mark or Dad. In a couple of years, she would be learning the game. However, it was with his sons that Dad was most concerned relative to tennis. Before long he would be getting us into matches and tournaments.

By the middle of the summer, I could beat Mark occasionally. When I beat him, I'd think I was just getting lucky, but he took it much more seriously. When he'd get angry and yell, I wasn't sure if his anger was directed at me or at himself. Before long, though, there was no mystery to his anger. It was directed at me. He seemed to explode with rage and hurled insults at me as well. He might have resented that I was now sharing time that formerly had been his alone with our dad. Later on, as we grew older, I realized it was more serious than that.

Both Mark and I took to the game with natural athletic ability and good form. We loved getting better and basked in Dad's approval and pride in us. We steadily improved under his instruction. We had an advantage that Dad didn't have because, when we were growing up, we had equal access to tennis courts any time of day. We were as proud of Dad's tennis accomplishments as he was of ours. We watched as he became the first-place winner of Mount Vernon's Tennis Tournaments for five straight years and won the Mansfield "News Journal Tournament." He was especially happy to be a champion in his hometown where as a child he was not given freedom to play on Mansfield's tennis courts – at least not in the daylight hours.

Most of our tennis improvement occurred when Mark and I played against each other. Because I had a heftier build and was more muscular, I was able to give Mark a lot of competition even though I was younger and had not played as long as he. I realize that it is hard to lose to a younger brother, but Mark's anger was starting to become a distraction to his game and to my focus. We played mostly at Riverside Park. During the first summer that I began playing competitive tennis, Mark became the Mount Vernon City Champion while I lost every game in the 12-and-under category.

This is a photo of Mom with a trophy won by my brother and me.

We were flattered that the nearby Kenyon College tennis coach, Bob Harrison, who knew my parents, became interested in Mark and me. He became a regular around our dinner table. Friends from Beatty Park Tennis in Columbus would also visit our house to play tennis and talk with Coach Harrison.

Soon Mark and I were good enough to play in tournaments around the area. When my dad recognized our tennis talents, he decided to take us to Columbus to play in bigger tournaments. Of course, tournament fees could be a problem at times, but Columbus was convenient, just an hour away from our house and the competition there was good for us. Playing in the Columbus area, however, turned out to be a disappointment as it would culminate in my second awareness of what I perceived as racism.

A few other blacks were playing in Columbus, but Mark and I stood out as the only blacks (except Al Matthews who lived there) who were playing in the Juniors Division in the tournaments. We began to win a few tournaments and started beating some of the better Columbus junior players. In addition to winning several Ohio Valley Tournament trophies, Dad would take us to other places such as Pennsylvania as family finances allowed. We started building a tennis reputation as ranking qualifiers in tough tournaments.

At the end of a particularly tough match when I, a twelve-year-old, had beaten a 16-year-old in the Columbus area, my opponent asked me questions about where I lived and what matches I had won. He told me that he had been taking lessons and playing tennis at a country club since he was five years old. I didn't know what a country club was, and he didn't know where Mount Vernon was. Still, I was flattered that he was talking to me since I was much younger. He pointed out a couple of things in my game that needed improvement and I felt good about his friendliness to me.

After many weeks, as our wins started to mount, Mark and I were told that we were playing "out-of-district" since we lived in Mount Vernon. We had learned about the Ohio Valley tournaments from our Beatty Park tennis friends and enjoyed traveling to the Columbus area, sometimes more than once a week in the summer. We had no idea at all that there were districting rules. Therefore, we were skeptical and shocked when informed that we could no longer play in the Columbus area, but would have to play tournaments in northeastern Ohio closer to Cleveland. This could have been racially motivated because stories spread that it was the parents of the kids we were beating who wanted us out of their district. Mark, Al and I were the only blacks in our division and we were winning most of the matches. We felt that we were being singled out and suspected that, if we had been losing on a regular basis, the districting issue may not have arisen. Whatever was the case, the reality is that we had to leave the area.

What is racism, though, and who is racist? Like beauty, it may be in the eye of the beholder. I am not certain that the redistricting decision was racially motivated, but it seemed so to Dad at the time. Still, I know how it felt when we were asked to leave. I felt hurt, disappointed and alienated. The feelings I had experienced in third grade after the kickball name-calling incident were re-visiting me.

Everyone sees life with a different set of eyes. I thought again about Dad's saying that we need to look beyond the obvious and see people for what they are on the inside. I began worrying, though, that maybe it was my fault that we were being asked to leave the Columbus area tennis matches. I wondered if it went back to my conversation with the sixteen-year-old who gave me the tips. I recalled two others boys who had talked with me after matches ended and asked me lots of questions. Maybe I had given out too much information about us and where we were from because I was eager to build friendships. I never discussed my anxiety with my dad or brother. I felt bad about what was happening because I was getting stronger as a player, benefiting from the tough competition provided in the Columbus area. At the time, though, we had no recourse except to leave.

My dad was upset in a practical way with the decision made by the Association because we lived less than an hour away from Columbus. Their decision would force us to drive two or three hours to play in tournaments in our "district." It meant not only more time, but also more wear and tear on the car, more gasoline and travel expenses. We wanted to fight the Association's decision but we had no money to hire a lawyer. The undercurrent was that some of the more influential parents did not want their kids beaten by two black brothers, and they had the clout to get us out. I was happy later when I learned that a few of the parents wanted us to stay and play in Columbus, but their numbers were smaller. I thought that the kinder parents may have been the parents of the kids with whom I had talked. They had seemed so nice! That thought made me feel a little better as we packed our tennis bags and headed to the Cleveland district.

When I was in the "14-and-Under" division I went to Kent State University to play in a tournament. Prior to our arriving on campus in May 1970, Kent State University students had demonstrated against America's involvement in the Vietnam War. Several students were shot and four were killed by National Guard troops. Tension on campus was high, and the atmosphere was surreal. National Guard troops dotted the campus like flies, and that included the tennis courts. Playing tennis next to men with M16s created an eerie atmosphere. They didn't put up with the usual misbehaving or swearing on the courts. The young offenders were pulled off the court and sent home. They certainly were tougher than any referee I'd ever had! The Kent State tournament marked the first time I experienced the division of our country over the Vietnam War.

Tennis was my conduit to the issues of the broader world. Small towns have a way of insulating you from the "outside" world. Our car trips to and from tournaments gave me a chance to talk about these things with my dad, and they afforded special time to bond with my dad and brother. It was during these talks that I learned about Rosa Parks and the Montgomery Bus Boycott that had occurred around the time of my birth. Dad also shared with me the words of Dr. Martin Luther King, Jr., who urged: "We must forever conduct our struggle on the high plain of dignity and discipline."

Beginning in 1967, Dad drove Mark and me from Mount Vernon to northern Ohio for tennis tournaments. As we drove back and forth, it was my dad's stories that helped me to come to terms with my anger about the tennis decision that led to our car trips. I decided that if my dad, who understood the nation's struggle and unrest could remain positive about his family's outlook and opportunities, I could too. Our problems dimmed in comparison as I learned about the Little Rock Nine who were barred from entering Central High School, despite the Brown vs. Board of Education lawsuit won by Thurgood Marshall that declared segregation in public schools unconstitutional.

This is a photo of Mark Jr., Mark, Sr. and me

I was shocked when Dad explained that James Meredith entered the University of Mississippi, but it took the protection of 5000 federal troops to control the vast mob. Dad went on to tell us about four black students from North Carolina Agricultural and Technical, a historically black college, who conducted a sit-in at a Woolworth's counter in the nearby town of Greenville, North Carolina. The courage of these students impressed me. Dad told us about the Freedom Riders, and I learned that Dr. King had been jailed in Birmingham in the spring and summer of 1963. It took Bull Conner, who called out the police dogs and fire hoses on the black demonstrators, to let America and the world know what had been going on. The stark and bloody images on television brought the scenes into the world's living rooms and shook everyone awake. However, because they thought we were too young, my parents sheltered us from those hateful images.

The drives to tennis tournaments awakened my awareness as Dad explained the lessons of the times which I had been too young to understand earlier. It was outlandish to learn that Medgar Evers, an NAACP field agent, in June of 1963 was murdered, but the murderer was freed by a hung jury—twice! (It took 30 years for him to be convicted.) A terrible sadness overcame me when I heard about the four little girls who died attending Sunday school in Birmingham when a bomb exploded in the church.

We did not rush onto the Columbus tournament scene, uninvited. We were not being aggressive. We entered tournaments there because the driving distance was convenient and the competition rigorous. In a tennis game you don't come in to try to take the net. You wait, instead, for the optimal time to come in. However, if we had waited for an "invitation," to participate in the Columbus tournaments, Mark and I would have been deprived of the growth we experienced through them. As I learned about the Civil Rights struggle, I understood that waiting for an "invitation" to claim their basic rights would have been much too costly for black Americans.   In tennis, if you come into the net uninvited, just because you want to take the net, you give your opponent more time to make a passing shot. In our case, as we headed north, the passing shot we heard was "good-by and move on."

CHAPTER THREE

Tennis Tip: Be ready for the unexpected. Always be alert and don't ever get complacent; because, even though in doubles you may not be involved immediately in the point, you may have to finish the point. One shot is sometimes all it takes to win the point, and you want that shot to be yours.

Mark's personality, which we noticed was beginning to change at the end of junior high, was even more alarming during his final two years of high school. He seldom had anything positive to say to me at a time when I was just starting high school and could have used his support. It wasn't just me, though. He was confrontational and argumentative with almost everyone. He had a hard time ever admitting he was wrong about anything. His obnoxious behavior may have been a screen to mask his own insecurities. Whatever the case, the constant drama was a drain on any semblance of family peace.

We were embarrassed frequently to see Mark nitpick with his girlfriend, Joan. He would criticize her clothes, for instance, and even the way she walked and talked. Since he was only 5' 7" in stature, we wondered if it may have been what people referred to as a "Napoleon" complex. It was astonishing to me to see Joan put up with his moods, but she did.

I remember one late summer afternoon when Mark brought Joan over to our house. Mom and I were shelling peas on the front porch when they walked up. We both looked up from our work and smiled, happy to see them. I was especially glad to see Joan. I must admit that I had a little crush on her. Joan was a beautiful, popular girl, the daughter of a minister. She always had a cheerful greeting for me; and I thought Mark was so lucky to have a girlfriend like her. I was also happy to be interrupted from the pea shelling and hoped they'd stay a long time and maybe offer to help us finish shelling them.

Before they could even get seated, though, Mark started out by saying, "You'll have to excuse Joan's raggedy jacket."

Mom said something like, "Joan looks beautiful in whatever she wears. I like the jacket, don't you, Steven?" I nodded affirmatively, and Joan just smiled.

Mark continued his criticism: "When I sat with Judy Scott at the volleyball game the other night, she wore a cute little denim jacket that I liked a lot. Joan ought to get one like Judy's."

Mark liked to let Joan know that he was paying attention to other girls, but he was quite jealous if Joan noticed other guys.

"Hey, Mark, you might think my clothes don't measure up, but there are other guys who seem to like the way I look" Joan said playfully.

Mark burst out with "What other guys?" balling up his fists as he yelled. I became concerned about where this conversation might be heading.

Joan jokingly replied, "Oh, too many to count."

At that point Mark grabbed the upper part of her right arm and turned her to face him. In a threatening voice, he snarled "I'd better never see you messing around with any other guys!"

He didn't punch her, as he had often punched me, but I could see how embarrassed and uncomfortable she became. He let go of her arm shortly and headed across the porch toward the swing.

I was embarrassed for Joan and inwardly thinking about how to deal with this when Mom interceded, as she often did, in an attempt to be a peacemaker. "Mark, she was just teasing. But, seriously now, how can you talk about going out with Judy Scott; yet get angry when Joan mentions other guys?"

Mark slumped down on the porch swing and muttered something like "Why are you all lined up against me?" I just shrugged my shoulders and rolled my eyes.

At that point Joan sat down gingerly on the edge of the porch swing. He glared at her and grumbled, "Don't try to get close to me after talking about all those other guys!" Joan only shook her head in reply.

Joan was a sweet-natured girl who tried to cajole him. She usually found ways to change the subject and humor him into a better mood. Mom, likewise, always seemed to appease Mark when he lashed out at others. In her typical way, Mom tried to lighten the mood. "I'll go inside and get us all something cold to drink. It's been such a hot day!"

She set down the bucket of peas that was in her lap and hurried inside to get the refreshments. However, as soon as she left, Mark took off with long strides across the lawn and down the street. Joan immediately ran after him, yelling for him to slow down so they could talk. He seemed to slow just a bit, and I saw her take his hand before they rounded the corner. I was so irritated that he could shoot off his mouth, ruin an evening, and get away with it. None of us had a clue at the time, however, that his rude behavior was symptomatic of a psychological condition beyond his control.

Most of the time I didn't have Mom and Joan's patience when he started picking on me. I just wanted his criticism to end, because Mark never passed up an opportunity to remind me that I was kind of "chunky" (his favorite nickname for me) and not really in shape. He never had a good word for me, and I couldn't please him no matter how much I tried. At times my father seemed to be part of a tag team with Mark to let me know what they thought of my physique. I don't know if Dad was also trying to appease Mark, or if he generally agreed with him. Either way, it hurt my feelings. So I sat there, thinking about all this, and shelled a few more peas as I waited for Mom to return.

When Mom came back with the soft drinks, she was disappointed that they had left. I said something like, "Some things never change." She sighed and sat down in the swing where Mark had been sitting. She slowly pushed the swing back and forth and said nothing more for awhile.

I was greedily downing my soft drink and saw that she had also brought potato chips. I was enjoying this unexpected treat until I realized that Mom hadn't even touched her cold drink or chips. She just sat there with a worried look on her face. She was a strong woman, not prone to weep or complain, but there was an unmistakable sadness in the way she sat and stared into the distance as if she could see trouble ahead.

"Steven, you go on out and hit tennis balls or whatever you'd like to do before darkness sets in. I'll finish up the peas."

I'm sure that my parents suspected some form of mental illness at work in Mark, but didn't want to confront it. It was easier to blame his behavior on outside circumstances or to overlook strange behavior at times until it became severe enough that it couldn't be denied. We knew that he was changing. What we thought previously was a short fuse or a hot temper was now much more than that. For instance, earlier in the summer, when he played poorly in a tennis match, he threw his racket and ended up chipping a tooth as a result of the racket boomeranging into his face. Mark's lack of court manners was outrageous to the degree that he would lose points in a match for his behavior.

If Mark's calling me "chunky" over and over was a psychological ploy to motivate me to get in shape, it worked. At the beginning of summer, I worked out and got into shape to stop him and Dad from making fun of me. Friends whom I had met in junior high were in a conditioning program for football in high school, so I frequently worked out with them. By late summer, I was considerably more muscular. I don't think either

Mark or Dad took any notice of my self-improvement plan until Mark and I got into our last fight.

His rage against me culminated one afternoon, just before school was to start. Mark and I were headed for the YMCA, and he was driving his Pinto. Out of nowhere he started to hassle me about losing a game several weeks before. His rage at me accelerated as did the speed of the Pinto. I was startled by the intensity of his insults, the raw language, and the recklessness with which he was driving. I spoke up for myself, though. "What the heck are you talking about? That's absolutely nuts!"

Hearing that, he abruptly pulled the car off the road and continued railing at me for "back-talking" him. I jumped out the passenger side of the door just as he was coming around to it. Off balance, I almost fell when he pushed me against the front fender. I quickly regained my balance and smacked him hard across the face.

Just as quickly as he had gotten out of the car, he turned around and got back into it. Jamming a heavy-metal 8-track into the tape player, he drove us to the YMCA as the music blared. Nothing was said about the fight, but he quit making fun of me and seemed to have some respect for my physical abilities as a result.

Still, Mark was my brother and I loved him. I was proud not only of his tennis but also his work in art.

He had many art pieces recognized at school and displayed around the building. Still-life and landscapes paintings in water colors and oils with an emphasis on impressionism appealed to his art teacher, and he was offered money for them. Because I admired my brother's art, I gave art a try in high school too. My art also was exhibited at Mount Vernon High School during my time there, and that made me happy.

I immediately made the boys' high school varsity tennis team at age 15. My brother was 17 at the time and already on the varsity tennis team. I started playing against high schools in the Columbus area. Mount Vernon High school's conference covered almost all of the schools around Columbus. I started playing against the same kids that Mark and I had competed against when I was younger before we were told to leave the Columbus area tournaments. I did quite well. During my junior and senior years, I went to the State Championships and won a few rounds. While all the tennis accomplishments were wonderful, I was concerned that my parents were divorcing. My dad moved to Newark, closer to his job, and eventually remarried. He remained close to us, however, and Mom was able to befriend his new wife as time moved onward.

My sister, Valerie, who was just finishing junior high at this time, was a volleyball star and also lettered in track and field, basketball and tennis. She was starting to be passionate about tennis as Mark and I had at that age. Kiersten, entering junior high, chose not to follow the sports tradition set by her older siblings. With Mom's encouragement and coaxing, she joined the local 4-H Club where she was taking cooking and sewing classes. Being artistic, she was achieving in those areas as early as age nine. Mom was continuing in her career as a secretary and trying to keep all of us on track in school and at home. Tennis for her was very occasional at this stage of her life.

My high school years were consumed with tennis. I think I hid behind the game because I had no social life. I dated very little because at this age the "race thing" always came up with parents. I was cautious about asking anyone for a date because I didn't want to be turned down. Adolescent insecurity is a problem even if race doesn't enter into the mix. Black girls just weren't around. Everywhere I looked I saw only white girls: at school, on television, and at social clubs. I wanted to date girls and enjoy the normal social events that high school kids enjoy – dances, proms, and other parties. Because white girls made up my pool of possibilities for dates, and I was afraid of the race thing, I did not date. Instead I concentrated on tennis almost exclusively for enjoyment and self-satisfaction. As I look back, I still feel a sense of loss for not having gone to a homecoming dance or prom, normal functions that I didn't feel secure enough to risk rejection or stir up racial anger by inviting a white girl to go with me.

I was pretty much of a loner because my best friends, Vincent and Charles, were football players and I wasn't. Even though I made waves in the tennis area, in high schools, then as now, football was the big social event on Friday nights, especially in small towns. No marching bands or cheerleaders spent time applauding or encouraging tennis. While Charles and Vincent were on the field, all suited up and looking good, I was just kind of walking around from one side of the football field to the other. I was not in the band, as Mark was, so the games were not a highlight for me. As I now look back, I find it sad that Vincent and Charles had possibly their only "glory days" while in high school. I've heard from the Mount Vernon grapevine that both have spent time in jail for drug dealing, and one was legally banned from the state of California.

At the beginning of my freshman year of high school, I took Kiersten and Valerie to a football game and, I'm sure, earned some "big brother points." My sisters reminded me, as we watched the game, that I had other athletic skills besides tennis. "You were the eighth grade ping pong champion in junior high!" While their admiration was sweet, it didn't take my mind off the fact that everyone else but me seemed to be having the time of their lives during Friday night football festivities in our small town. I felt like an outsider and the feeling brought me down.

I did stick my neck out once in the fall of my sophomore year. It was a Saturday after one of those Friday night football games. The fall afternoon was cool and crisp, and I had girls on my mind. I got "spiffed up" and set out to the bowling alley outside Mount Vernon. A social club it was called. I was feeling especially social and itching to talk to a couple of girls who had given me a certain look on Friday afternoon at the pep rally. The girls had giggled about the fact that they were going to the social club on Saturday, but they made sure that I knew where it was and at what hour the socializing would begin.

I spent about an hour or more deciding whether I should wear jeans or khakis and what kind of shirt, polo or sport shirt. Being careful not to be noticed by any of my family, I locked myself in our one-and-only bathroom to pick and re-pick my Afro. I was going, no doubt about it; and I wasn't telling anyone in my family that I was going. I didn't want to have to answer any questions or take any teasing. I had practiced how I was going to enter the social club, with kind of a swagger.

As I swaggered in, there sat the girls in a booth in the middle of the room, trying not to be caught noticing me as I tried not to give the appearance that I was looking for them.

After a couple of minutes of this cat-and-mouse game, I strolled over to them. They offered me a Coke, and we sat in the booth and chatted. They sat on one side and I sat on the other. I began to relax and crack a few jokes. They were giggling at my jokes, as we munched on pretzels and sipped Cokes. My social powers seemed to be working better than I imagined. All my planning and preparation seemed to be paying off.

Then, in a shivering second it ended. The scene abruptly turned scary when five guys, whom I had seen watching me while I was talking to the girls, cornered me and began yelling racial slurs. The girls' faces turned to stark fear as they remained in the booth while I got up. One of the men, who appeared to be older than my brother, grabbed my Coke bottle and hit me in the face with it. When you are cornered five to one, it is not smart to be a hero. Escape is the only tactic to employ. With Coke pouring down my face and neck and dripping onto my good shirt, adrenalin pumped me up. I jumped over a couple of chairs and managed to get out the door ahead of them. They stopped chasing me after I got to the parking lot. I looked over my shoulder to see that they had planted themselves beside the large bowling alley sign. They stood there laughing at me and continued their racial slurs which quickly faded into the wind behind me.

My running speed had again paid off. I was able to sneak into the house after dark and wash the sticky soda off my skin and my shirt. The bruise on my face from the impact of the bottle remained for a few days. The embarrassment that I felt whenever I saw the girls at school lasted much longer. My hope for a social life in high school died that night. Tennis was it, my one and only social satisfaction in high school. I did find satisfaction in science in high school. Even though reading continued to be a downfall for me, I was enthralled with science and especially liked the labs. The country's interest in outer space had captivated my attention as well and I delved into science with enthusiasm.

My mother's constant lessons in optimism seemed to take root in me. I reflected on her statement that you can't achieve anything by blaming your failures on other people's prejudice. You have to work and try to solve your problems by staying positive. "You can't change others," she would say. "The only person you can change is yourself."

Although I didn't talk with her or any of the family about the incident, I took a positive and preventive step in dealing with bullies. I used all the money I could get my hands on to buy every Bruce Lee karate book I could find. By reading the books and following the illustrations, I taught myself karate. My natural athleticism and perseverance in karate helped me in tennis. Later on I would come back to karate when facing problems in college. Even more important than the training in self-defense, I learned self-confidence and self-reliance. I would need it even more, I thought, as my brother was heading off to Kent State University on an athletic scholarship in tennis. Even though he had been hard to get along with and unpredictable, I would miss not having him around.

My brother had never talked with me much about dating and neither had my dad. Mark had been fully engaged in the high school rituals of dating, proms, homecoming dances and the rest. He had figured out how to date and still stay alive and healthy in Mount Vernon. His white girlfriend was the daughter of a pastor, and her family had no problem at all accepting Mark, a minority kid, light-skinned, good looking, and socially successful. Mark not only was an outstanding athlete, he was an excellent watercolor artist and took awards as a member of the high school marching band. During my first two years in high school, I used to wish I was more like him, and I envied his popularity.

Mark was glib, articulate, smooth talking and charming. I was just the opposite. I became tongue-tied, stuttered and stammered when I tried to turn on the charm. Being self-conscious at the time, I was shy about bringing up with Mark the topic of dating and the problems I had encountered when I tried to date. I recall, though, asking him about dating his girlfriend's younger sister who was my age and a really pretty girl. Mark didn't think that was a good idea because, even though he was accepted by his girlfriend's family, he didn't want to push the envelope. I was disappointed, of course, but not surprised because I felt that it was logical that he wouldn't stick his neck out for me. It reinforced in me the notion that I didn't measure up, that in his eyes I was still "Chunky."

The fear that I might be teased or belittled by him overrode my desire to ask him for any help. I felt safer leaving the dating subject under the rug and sharing only those things that might make me look strong in his eyes. I learned all I could from him and Dad about tennis as we continued to practice together and drive to tournaments. I am glad that Mark was able to enjoy all aspects of high school, because after high school his world would start to unravel.

During a tennis game you want to stay focused and never take your eye off the ball. You want the winning shot to come from your racket. I decided there was no dating focus for me in Mount Vernon. Because a successful social life in high school for me seemed to be a low-percentage game, filled with unforced errors and danger, I walked away from the dating game and devoted myself to the game in which I could succeed.

CHAPTER FOUR

Tennis Tip: On every tennis shot you should try to turn. Turning your body is vital to finishing your shot and putting balls away, both volleys and ground strokes.

Mark's behavior was changing, and the changes were now quite frightening. I didn't realize the extent to which these changes would limit his accomplishments; even the very length of his life. As I look back I realize he was becoming a different person from the one I had looked up to most of my life. For example, I recall a time when I was entered at a higher level (which is called "playing up") in a tournament, and my brother and I got to the finals. I let Mark win because he needed to look good in order to get the scholarship to Kent State. I was shocked to see that he was totally self-consumed as he boasted about his skill and my poor performance. He seemed to delight in making me look weak. Even though he had teased me when I was younger, this behavior was unexpected, startling, but most of all sad. In spite of his outstanding gifts in art and music, or maybe because of them, Mark started to develop an attitude that people "owed him." He felt that he never got all the accolades he deserved. That attitude was a harbinger of worse things to come his way.

Since Mark went to Kent State University on an athletic scholarship in tennis, I naturally hoped the door would be open for me as well. In high school I had won first-place singles in the Ohio Capitol Conference three years in a row. At the state of Ohio tennis championships I qualified twice and won some matches my junior and senior years.

Now that Mark was away at college, Dad's attention started to focus solely on me and my tennis ability which thrilled me. In Mark's absence, I became the number one player at Mount Vernon High School. Mark still competed in area tennis matches, but more and more of his attention began to focus on music. He began playing gigs in any group that would have him, in particular on the east side of Columbus. As he began to acquire recognition for his musical prowess, he started giving school less attention. Mom suspected that he was using recreational drugs, an activity that often accompanied rock bands at that time. That marked the beginning of his eventual collapse. He had a few out-of-state gigs with local bands, but became increasingly tormented that he was not getting the attention he deserved. When he didn't get the "star" adulation that he felt was his due, Mark became restless and dissatisfied. He was a willing participant in the "if it feels good, do it" thinking of the 70s. He'd try anything that might make him feel better, if not superior.

In addition to playing tennis in the fall, spring and summer when the weather would permit, I practiced in Columbus at the Joyce Avenue Indoor Tennis Club which was a private club where you could play as long as you had the money to pay for it. I could only afford to go on Sunday nights, but it did help when Dad could get me there. I like to think that playing at Joyce Avenue helped position me for playing Davis Cup the summer after my senior year of high school. That opportunity definitely increased my visibility.

In the summer after my junior year in high school, I went to Kent State and ended up qualifying for the Westerns. I played tournaments in Parma, Elyria, and other places in northeastern Ohio in the 16 and 18 year-old singles category. I was ranked number one for two years in a row in northern Ohio. Those victories gave me some "bragging rights" as I was getting ready for college. At a Wittenberg tournament, I was on the bus with Vitas Gerulaitis and Francis Gonzales. It turned out that Gonzales was my teammate. Later in life, he went on the pro circuit and beat such notables as Ivan Lendl and Jimmy Connors from time to time. Without a financial sponsor, going on the pro circuit was impossible for me, but I've always wondered where I might have gone if I had had a sponsor and could have joined Gonzales. I was well aware that my best bet was getting a college education and later a job to support myself, so I stayed on track and focused on getting good enough to be considered for a college tennis team.

My big break came when I was in high school playing in a tournament against the top player for The Ohio State University. The match was very close and I lost, but the OSU coach, John Daly, was impressed with my playing and told my mother I could be a walk-on for his team. My high school counselor had recommended that I go to a vocational school and told my mother that, "We all know Steve is a great class clown and has a keen sense of humor, but he's not too serious about his education."

The sad fact is that I was concerned about my education, but embarrassed to read aloud in front of others. Even today I get nervous if I am called on to read aloud. One time in sixth grade, when the teacher asked me to read aloud, I was nervous but doing the best

I could. Kids in the back started laughing at me and making fun of me. Instead of showing embarrassment, I joined in the silliness, although I was cringing inside. Any time I am asked to read aloud, my mind goes back to that scene. Reading is one of the most important skills, and it was my biggest challenge. Starting in third grade, I did not perform up to par because of my problem in learning to read. Each year I was passed on to the next grade, but I couldn't keep up with the work.

Today they put students with reading deficiencies in special classes. Even then, they may have in other districts, but I was in Amity, Ohio, and that did not happen. Being ashamed that I was not at grade level in reading, I tried to hide it through my sense of humor, thereby earning the "class clown" label. Through hard work and determination, I was able to advance, but what I needed early in my school life was tutoring help. People have told me that by third grade a child is either reading or not reading at the appropriate level, and if help isn't given then, reading becomes an academic handicap thereafter, and that was the case for me. The little country school in Amity where I spent my formative years as a student kept all the students together and did nothing for the "class clowns" except discipline them for interrupting the class.

That remark – that I was not college material – was just the kind of write-off that can evoke an "I'll show you!" attitude from me – or maybe the counselor was using reverse psychology. Whatever the case, I was college bound, whether the counselor saw it or not. I made the big move to Columbus and started college at OSU in 1974. I was quite scared, though, because entrance testing showed that my reading level was at the tenth grade. I was more than scared; I was terrified, because I couldn't imagine getting a college degree with my reading handicap. Ohio State was good in offering "study tables" to help kids like me, and I never missed a session. In reality I don't know how much the study tables helped, but I did my part in showing up and taking advantage of any help I could get - from anyone - in order to pass the courses.

Valerie and Kiersten were proving to be strong in academics. The summer before I started my college career was a good one for Valerie who had won a Teen Magazine writing contest about the *Jackson Five*. The other national winner was from Anaheim, California. Valerie's prize was a trip to Los Angeles that included taking Mom with her, all expenses paid. The timing of the trip was perfect because she was just getting over a summer romance with a fifteen-year-old boy whose mother discouraged it.

While Mom and Valerie were off to California, Dad was taking young Kiersten to Beatty Park to play tennis with the group there. Kiersten, like the rest of us before her, was finding that tennis was the item that got attention from Dad. He signed her up in tournaments and recommended that she get more aggressive as they went to Beatty once or twice a week.

While I was entering Ohio State, Mark was being kicked out of Kent State. His "extra- curricular" pursuits in Columbus clubs and dives, added to his relentless search for whatever it took to make him feel superior, came crashing down on him. Even his artwork had transformed into violent outbursts of jagged and disconnected lines, abstract to the point of insanity. Our worst fears about Mark's emotional changes over the years had been realized when Mark was diagnosed as schizophrenic. He had been at Kent State only two years before he was kicked out for not attending classes, letting grades slip, and failing in every area. Not even tennis, which had gotten him there, mattered to him. His attitude of entitlement not only ended his college career, but resulted in his being fired from almost every job he got after he left Kent State.

Being concerned with my own issues at OSU, I was unaware that schizophrenia was the prevailing cause of Mark's unpredictable behavior. I knew that schizophrenia meant a split personality, and I remembered how changeable his moods had been. It remains upsetting to our family that, because he was away at Kent State and we were involved in our own lives, none of us realized that he needed psychiatric help. Mark was using alcohol and other drugs to the extent that any pharmaceuticals (e.g. lithium) that might control the schizophrenia were ineffective.

While I was adjusting to college life at Ohio State and Mark was completely out of control, it was comforting to know that my sisters were doing all right. Valerie was on the tennis team at Mount Vernon High and playing well which made Mom and Dad happy. She was also in choir and became the second black majorette at Mount Vernon High School. We were so proud of her. Kiersten, who was in middle school, was illustrating outstanding scholarship. Although she was focused primarily on academics, she also was becoming an excellent tennis player. Dad was spending time instructing her and Valerie, as he had done with Mark and me.

This is a photo of Valerie, the 2nd African-American
high school majorette in our little town.

Shortly after leaving Kent State, Mark began playing with various bands, doing gigs all over the central Ohio area. He was playing at Alexandria, a bar on the east side of Columbus, when Mom received a phone call that indicated he was spinning out of control. When she caught up with him, she discovered that he was creating "star charts" reminiscent of the Russell Crowe movie, *A Beautiful Mind,* in which a famous mathematician who suffered from schizophrenia decorated the walls of his garage with intricate mathematical formulas which made sense only to him.

Mom was able to get Mark to return to Mount Vernon and get back on track with his medication, at least for a little while. He even landed a great job in the Big Brothers Association, director of the organization in Mount Vernon. However, he didn't keep the position for long because his behavior got in the way.

After returning from a conference in Michigan, he was impatient with the status of the Mount Vernon office and wanted to see the office there, under his direction, compare more favorably. This is where Mark's judgment comes to question. Instead of going through the chain of command and trying to brainstorm and problem solve with others, he took it upon himself to criticize others and ridicule the slowness of their ideas. He called Mount Vernon's Big Brothers Association backward and "country bumpkin" in comparison with Detroit's. Mark made outlandish demands for change, and when he was confronted with reality, ranted: "You guys are so 'backward'" or words to that effect. The result was that he was fired from the job. Mark had great ideas, but he wanted things to happen as fast as his mind could imagine them. The problem was that his mind, though creative, imaginative and open to change, was out of focus and his thoughts were racing far beyond reality. The Big Brothers job would have been a wonderful career step for him if he had possessed the self-discipline, patience, and humility to work with others to bring about the change that he knew was needed.

It wasn't long after that episode when Mom got a call from the Mount Vernon police that Mark had been picked up in Riverside Park, the site where we had spent so many hours playing tennis. Because he was chanting and hallucinating, the police suspected that he was on drugs. Whether or not he was, we don't know. However, that experience sent him packing for Columbus and other musical gigs. He never had any trouble getting a job with a band because he was so musically gifted, especially on the drums. However, he was not in a position to build a future on his musical talent, and tennis was a memory for him. My family kept a lot of this from me at the time because I had my own struggles adjusting to life at Ohio State.

The college experience proved to be a real culture shock to me because it was the first time in my life that I was living among black people other than my family. I discovered what may be shocking to many white people: that blacks can experience culture shock from blacks! Even though that may sound absurd, I can assure you it was real because in my growing- up experiences I had been more involved in the white culture and had not learned the social behaviors of blacks. Black students there didn't know what to make of me.

I discovered that culture shock is independent of skin color. I didn't know how to respond to blacks who would say, "What's happenin'" or "How ya' doin'" when they saw me crossing the oval. The fact that I didn't know them at all seemed irrelevant to them. However, I thought, just as my white friends did, that it was strange they would greet me in such a friendly way without knowing me. They appeared overbearing to me, and I became immediately suspicious of their brash behavior.

"Oreo" is used sometimes by blacks to put down other blacks. Calling a black person "Oreo" is saying that he is trying to be something other than what he really is. My rural, small-town roots among whites produced my behavior and made me "white" on the inside; while my outside appearance was closer to black. The fact is that I was not in control of either the inside or outside. My adjustment to college was challenging because of this dichotomy of culture and race.

I tried to understand why it was that I was having a hard time being accepted by my race. When I took an introductory psychology course, I latched on to a concept called imprinting. The idea of imprinting made as much sense to me as anything else to explain why I was tied to the white race more than the black one. The idea of imprinting came about in a study concerning baby ducks. Immediately after they are hatched, baby ducks instinctively follow the mother duck. That is referred to as "imprinting" behavior. In an experimental study it was found that, in the absence of a mother duck, the ducklings will follow a mechanical duck or other object. After the initial behavior is learned, and they have been successfully "imprinted," the ducklings know no difference between a live, mother duck and a mechanical duck.

The course made me reflect about my behavior in growing up. I wondered if I had been "imprinted" to follow white behavior. If that had happened, maybe it explained my predicament in relating to other blacks. It dawned on me that I had to work on adapting to the mannerisms of the black culture in order to broaden my experiences and eventually be accepted by blacks.

I learned to adapt, yet adapting was temporary. I could not authentically become something I was not. When a black guy would come up to me and start talking to me in what I perceived to be a too-familiar way, I wouldn't try to fake a "black" reply. I would answer in my own language, even if I was being perceived as "acting white." I answered sincerely and with respect for the black culture to which I also belonged; but never tried to fake it to fit in. Even though I couldn't change my intrinsic make-up, I was able to develop rapport with blacks in order to navigate more easily from one group to another after awhile. Because I felt insecure at times in the Ohio State setting (not unusual for any rural kid going to one of the largest universities in the country) and unsure of myself socially with new white and black friends, I reached back to the help I had found in karate when I was in high school. I took classes in judo and kung fu at OSU; and, as before, these classes helped me build new self-confidence and assurance. An added benefit was a second-degree black belt.

Even today there is a real shortage of black students at Ohio State, especially black males. In the 1970s, black students were rare. Consequently, they were more likely to band together because of the scarcity. My outward appearance led black students to assume that I was raised with black influences, when that was actually far from reality. I found that blacks at Ohio State had a brotherhood that I could not quite understand nor fit into. As a result, I really did not have many black friends. The blacks whom I met in class kidded me for the way I spoke. I didn't have the street talk that most of them possessed, so they thought I was "trying" to talk and be white. I realized I was thinking like a white man who was placed in a black body. Ultimately this led to my feeling out of place at Ohio State, just as I had at home in Mount Vernon. Fortunately, after the first year it became easier; but, during that first year, I would not have believed that it would ever feel right.

The first year proved to be the hardest in other ways, too, as I was finding my way. The Ohio State tennis team was represented largely by privileged kids. Some of them drove cars that cost more than my parents' house in Mount Vernon. I discovered that what was eye-boggling to me, such as owning a car at 16, was normal to them. John, one of my tennis friends, drove a Porsche. When I expressed admiration and amazement, he shirked it off by saying it was a high school graduation present. I thought that a wristwatch or a nice pen-and pencil set was the standard gift. It was clear that John lived in a different world, and I was eager to learn all I could about it. Their clothes were another impressive feature. I recalled a popular saying: "Clothes make the man." I don't think the guys on the tennis team and I shopped at the same J.C. Penney's. Thinking along that same vein, I tried to put things into perspective by applying the saying to tennis; i.e. "Porsches produce tennis players." I immediately grinned to myself as I saw how ridiculous that sounded. I couldn't help being dazzled by the car, but knew in my heart that your value lies in what you become, not in what you are given. I would try to remain focused on what I might become as a result of attending Ohio State and not let material things that I did not possess get me down. I felt confident that one day I would be able to dress and drive in a manner that was comparable to most of my tennis friends. I also knew then, as now, that no matter how rich you get, there's always going to be somebody richer.

Charles, one of my black friends from Mount Vernon, was assigned as my roommate. What a nice surprise that was. Later, however, I learned that we didn't have much in common at Ohio State since I spent so much time with the tennis team and worked hard with the tutor in my free time to keep up with my grades. Unfortunately, in spite of Charles' education at private schools as we were growing up together in Mount Vernon, he flunked out of Ohio State after only one quarter. He, like many other freshmen, got caught up in the social freedom away from home and made some bad decisions in choosing friends. He started on a course from which he didn't turn back. I learned that he became part of the drug scene, advancing from user to dealer. The last I heard was that he was in jail. Learning from his bad decisions and turning away from those who were pulling him in the wrong direction was something he somehow was not willing to do.

In the '60s a group called The Byrds appeared on the Ed Sullivan Show and later captured a number-one place in folk music with a ballad written by Pete Seeger, "Turn, Turn, Turn." The lyrics go like this: "To everything (turn, turn, turn) there is a season (turn, turn, turn) and a time to every purpose under heaven. A time to be born, a time to die; a time to love, a time to hate; a time for peace; I know it's not too late." Seeger took the beautiful book of Ecclesiastes, chapter 3, from the Bible and paraphrased the words, adding only the last line about peace. In reflecting upon those stirring words, along with the turbulence of the Vietnam War and the Civil Rights movement, I realize that I, too, was "turning" and adjusting in trying to find my purpose and place in the world.

My teammates respected me despite my lack of "things" and we got along. I understood where they came from, and they understood my background as well. I also understood where they were going – to a fraternity that would not have accepted me because of my race, even if I had the money to join. We crossed paths as I emerged from my dorm and they came off the lawn of their fraternity house. A few of them formed a "mock fraternity" with me.

When I had the privilege of going home from school occasionally, Mom and I would talk about Mark. She and I were both disappointed that Mark had left tennis behind completely when he found that he could make money easily by playing in bands at clubs, and he liked that. Mark had innate musical talent and could always get gigs in bands in college and after he was kicked out of college. There is little doubt that he used drugs and alcohol when he played with bands, but his problems went beyond substance abuse. We suspected that his gifts might have contributed to his downfall. I have read that highly sensitive and gifted people may have a harder time focusing on one area, because of their many gifts. As for his musical abilities, one of his fellow musicians remarked to Mom that "Mark could make those drums walk and talk. His beat was so compelling that those drums would seem to come and get you. You'd get really wrapped up in their spell."

As we tried to figure out how Mark had lost his way, we decided that it was unfortunate that he had several gifts competing for his attention. Maybe he could have centered on one as a profession and the others as a hobby. It is painful to look back on those days from the perspective of an adult, and to realize that the serious emotional and psychological changes occurring inside Mark were going to have such a devastating effect on his life. When schizophrenia took command during that dark time of his life, I became the supportive big brother to him that I had always wanted him to be for me.

In the summer of 1975, after my first year at Ohio State, Mark called me and wanted to come and see me at school. During summers at Ohio State, I worked as a camp counselor for the National Youth Sports Program in which tennis pros help under-privileged school kids who are needy. I liked it from the start, and over the coming summers I came to realize that sports recreation was the perfect major for me. I knew that I would be happy teaching tennis as a career as I gained satisfaction from watching kids learn. I was living in the dorms near the tennis camp location when Mark called to say that he was traveling through Columbus and wanted to catch up with me.

We met at The Library, a popular campus bar. I was shocked by his bedraggled and thin appearance. He looked like an outline of his former self. After we ordered, he began to tell me about his prospective job, the destination that was taking him through Columbus. If I was shocked at his appearance, I was beyond shock as I listened to him describe his job as we sat in a booth eating cheeseburgers. Between bites he stated "I will be piloting a Lear Jet for Jackie Onassis." She was the widow of President John F. Kennedy who married Aristotle Onassis, a Greek billionaire, after Kennedy's assassination. As I was catching my breath, Mark switched quickly to a British dialect. He was becoming increasingly hard to understand as his delusional behavior played out. After I got him to leave the bar with me, we walked to my dorm room. Mark crashed as soon as he lay down on my bed.

After I saw that Mark was down for the evening, I phoned Mom to share what had occurred at the restaurant and to let her know that Mark was safe with me. She told me that she was not surprised because he had used the British accent with her. She went on to divulge that he had put together an intricate chart that resembled astrological signs. He created and named his signs. The chart design was highly intricate, but understandable only to Mark. The Lear Jet and the chart, she said, were predictable signs that he was slipping into a schizophrenic state. I would hear a lot more about the chart the next day and many days to come as Mark slept in my room.

He came and went that summer in and out of my dorm room. In the fall my dorm assignment switched, and I was relocated to another building, but Mark kept sleeping in the old room until I had to tell him to move on. He moved back to Mount Vernon at that time. Because of his superb musical talent, he continued to get stints in pick-up bands and did other odd jobs, flittering from one to another, never keeping a job for long. Mom had a full-time job of rescuing Mark from one catastrophe to another.

Both Mark and I knew the tennis maxim about the need to turn. By turning – in tennis as in life – one adjusts, prepares, and puts oneself in the correct position to complete a successful shot and win the point. As a young college student consumed with my own cares and aspirations for the future, I still was filled with dread and keenly aware that Mark might be turning into a downward spiral never to recover.

CHAPTER FIVE

Tennis Tip: Hit the ball "low-to-high." This means hitting the bottom part of the ball in order to create top spin. Hitting the ball low-to-high keeps you in control and keeps your ball in the court.

I owe a lot to Ohio State. I not only received a good education there, but without the financial assistance which later became a scholarship, I would have had only one other option available immediately after high school which was enlisting in the United States Army. Although I was not attracted to the military at the time, I was seeking a career with a future. The Army would have provided me with better career possibilities than I could have attained with a job that required only a high school degree.

As it was, though, with Pell grants and other financial aid which my mom was able to arrange for me, I was able to pay for tuition, room and board at Ohio State. The university arranged other work-study assistance, such as cleaning up the stadium on Sundays after the Saturday Buckeye games. I was happy for the extra money, but the job was odious. The foul smell of garbage still comes to mind when I first begin to think about Ohio State football games and the "Shoe," which the stadium is called.

In college I was most concerned with taking care of business: the business of tennis, which got me there; but, more importantly, the business of keeping up my grades in order to stay there. I was eager to take any assistance offered to keep my grades acceptable. My major was Recreation Education, and my goal was to be a professional tennis instructor. I wanted to help others gain the skills and satisfaction of tennis. A secondary goal for me, as a young person, was to make friends and enjoy the college life. I was eager to gain the social life, including dating, which I had lacked in high school.

As my sophomore year began at OSU, I was continuing to adjust between the two worlds of white and black. Unfortunately, I discovered that there could be dissension and resentment within the black community when all blacks didn't fit the black stereotype. Bill Cosby, a black entertainer and TV star, received backlash for his ongoing lectures that called on black parents to own up to their responsibility and get the point across to their kids that they needed an education to succeed. He asked them not to expect success and entitlement to be handed to them because their ancestors were slaves. Hard work was the key.

"It's time to stop using that excuse as a crutch and stop thinking a quick buck can be made on the streets listening to the drug guys" to paraphrase his message. It is still common today for black kids who make an effort to better themselves by going to school and getting an education to be "ragged on" by the guys in the "hood." The guys in the street claim that a trade-off is necessary. The "successful" blacks, they claim, are those who "try to be white" and sell out to the white culture. It seems that they don't see the inherent insult in that claim – i.e. that "acting black" leads to a lack of success, or failure.

Cosby was criticized by members of the black community for his opposition to name-calling and foul language in rap music, especially the use of the "n" word and words that denigrated women. In my opinion Cosby was right. I would later get a chance at OSU to play tennis with Bill Cosby.

While growing up in a small town with very few blacks, I accepted the fact that people had to put in the necessary work to succeed at whatever path they chose. My mom and dad preached that being a minority meant you had to try harder to gain recognition, and that everything minorities do stands out. They elaborated on that as a warning that everything bad that minorities do stands out even *more*. They taught me to be proud of being a minority by projecting positive actions and accomplishments; by putting forth the effort necessary to achieve. I was taught to believe I was "unique" rather than "different" and those lessons stuck.

The lessons of my parents about being black were reinforced at Ohio State the summer my sister, Valerie and I attended a seminar led by my hero and role model, Arthur Ashe. Mr. Ashe impressed me because, in addition to his outstanding tennis career, he was so smooth and genteel in manner. I don't recall the complete context of his message, but I came away with a determination to put up with whatever was necessary – whether it was cleaning up garbage after football games, racial slurs, or anything else – in order to reach my lifetime goals of graduating from college and entering a satisfying job. I could see the lights go on with Valerie also as we sat in that auditorium hanging onto every word.

Ashe advanced race relations by his quiet dignity. His pride in his heritage compelled him to believe that blacks did not need special treatment, such as Affirmative Action which was passed when Lyndon

Johnson was president in 1965. The plan refers to policies that take factors like "race, color, religion, sex or national origin" into consideration in order to benefit an underrepresented group, usually as a means to counter the effects of a history of discrimination. Not only did Mr. Ashe think it was a bad idea, but also he felt Affirmative Action was an insult because it could be viewed as black deficiency. He did not make his points in a fiery way, such as the Black Panthers and other groups were prone to do. He spoke softly and with reason. He assured us that whites did not have a monopoly on tennis or academics. Exposure to opportunity, he was convinced, would prove excellence. The only deficit of blacks and other minorities was the lack of opportunity. Once that level playing field was established – by hard work and sacrifice – Ashe was convinced that there would be no ceilings on achievement by the black race.

Arthur Ashe spoke of his growing up in the segregated south and his move to the University of California at Los Angeles for college. In spite of his tennis success at U.C.L.A., he explained to the audience, he wasn't allowed at that time to play tennis on the courts at the University of Richmond (Virginia), his hometown. However, he refused to let racial prejudice be a barrier to his progress. He spoke of college friendships and shared the fact that he was held at arm's length by his white college friends. They were friendly; but, because of racial tension and customs of the day, he was never invited into their houses. We imagined lonely times for him during Thanksgiving and Christmas holidays.

He shared his love of music and the arts with us. We knew about his tennis, but we didn't know that he had been in band during junior and senior high school. He spoke of art which, he explained "came from an urge as primal as survival itself." My mind drifted to my brother, Mark, at that point in Mr. Ashe's lecture. For him, art had served a primal need or so it seemed to me.

On race, Arthur Ashe felt that many people in the world still see color as an obstacle or deficiency, and he admitted that he could become angry and disappointed when, because of racial stereotypes, a worthy man or woman could be passed over for a position. At the same time, he admitted that he could become equally frustrated when an unworthy person cries "racism" when denied a position or a prize in a fair competition. He continued to remind us that he couldn't tolerate an "entitlement" mindset. Mr. Ashe, who had grown up under racism, and the laws of segregation, remained hopeful. Racism and sexism, he told us, will not go away with legislation. It is up to all of us to rise above the "isms."

In order to make it at Ohio State, I had to work hard and remain positive. Some black athletes at Ohio State assumed I was from California because I played tennis. Most athletes from the Midwest played what they referred to as the "traditional" black sports such as football or basketball. They were not used to seeing a black athlete carrying a handful of rackets into the Woody Hayes practice facility, but they were cool with it.

Playing on the tennis team was an honor, and undoubtedly one of the greatest experiences I've ever had. But even here I felt like the "odd man out" not because I was black, but because everybody else on the team came from wealth and privilege, or at least that seemed to be the case. One of the things that separated us was that I had never had a tennis lesson from a "pro" in my life. On the other hand, my teammates grew up playing at tennis clubs, including year-long practice and play at indoor courts, under the direction of a pro. My tennis experience had depended on good weather which is limited in the Midwest. Sometimes, when I was having a bad day, I felt they might be thinking, "Who are you to think you can play with us? You're only a walk-on!" The work ethic instilled in me by my parents helped me prove myself. By playing to my ability, I eventually earned the respect of the college tennis team regardless of our differences in wealth, social status, or race.

My dad was amazing to me as an example of one who was totally accepting of all races. Even though he had suffered extreme prejudice during the 1940s while growing up in Mansfield, he had learned early in life how to stay safe and make his own way. He was never into a "gang," but he had figured out that it was safer to band together with friends, and I think that was a smart and positive way to avoid conflict. It is much easier for trouble makers, he told me, to attack a single kid when they are looking to prove to themselves, that they are "all that and a bag of chips." I recalled my experience in high school when I had been attacked by several guys, and knew he was right. However, he was convinced that they are not so bold when attacking a group, especially a group minding their own business. I remembered those lessons from my dad while I was at Ohio State, although my problems with racial discrimination were few because of my light skin color. In fact, I found it easier to fit in with whites than with blacks, and Dad would see that as ironic.

When I went home for winter break during my sophomore year I found that Valerie, who was a high school senior at the time, had been running marathons. She was involved in basketball and track, as well as tennis, and planned to go out for softball in the spring. Mom said that Valerie planned to attend Ohio State. Kiersten was turning out to be a good volleyball player and was still at the top of her class academically. My brother, Mark, was doing odd jobs around Mount Vernon with an occasional gig playing drums in local bars. I knew that Mom had to get him out of scrapes from time to time and was uneasy in regard to Mark, always waiting for the "other shoe to fall". Since Dad lived in Newark, most of the responsibility for Mark, who lived with Mom in Mount Vernon, was in Mom's lap.

I was relatively happy with my life when I returned to Ohio State in January. I felt accepted by my teammates on the tennis court, yet I was not asked to pledge the fraternity they joined. No blacks were in that fraternity. There was a black fraternity at OSU, but I did not think I would fit in there either. My best friends were white guys on the track team, and at one point, six of us lived in an apartment off campus, and I was the only African-American in the group. No bunch of fraternity guys had more fun! One of those buddies and I still enjoy a close relationship. He travels the world on business, and a few years back treated me to a vacation in Taiwan. I like to use this example of a lasting friendship when I talk with young folks today about racial conflict or what they may suspect to be racial conflict. You will most likely win when you give people the benefit of the doubt rather than holding onto assumptions that can't be proven.

Tennis is what got me through the door at Ohio State, and my game continued to improve as I reached out to the black tennis community at Beatty Tennis Courts in the area around East High School which is a rough urban neighborhood. Some of the older black players, many of them professional men, reached out to me and became interested in my tennis game. When I would go out there, mostly on weekends to play, many of them remembered me from the days when Dad took Mark and me to Beatty when we were twelve and fourteen. They seemed proud of the fact that I was in college and made me feel special. I appreciated their friendship and it got me away from campus where I could associate with a group that knew my family. With their encouragement and my positive attitude of hard work, I remember the days in college as some of the best of my life.

Ohio State classes, as well as a social life, gave me additional insight into my future possibilities. One of my favorite classes was geology. I had liked science from an early age, and I found this particular teacher of geology to be the best teacher of my life. He made the study of rocks so much fun. His lectures were lively, and learning was easy because of it. I had never been so motivated to study and perform as I was in that class. In addition to his teaching talents, he understood my tennis schedule and the need to miss lectures at times when the tennis team was away for games. He would let me make up the work I had missed. He displayed my picture on the bulletin board of his classroom when Ohio State's student newspaper, *The Lantern*, published an article about tennis with a huge photo of me in the piece. His encouragement was significant for me at the time because I was not a confident scholar.

Meeting people from all over the country and other parts of the world opened up my world, especially the world of dating possibilities. The open-minded aspect of college life made dating women from other backgrounds easier. Tennis also opened my world view in that I had never traveled up to that point. The trips we took as a tennis team exposed me to a wide array of experiences. I must admit I wasn't crazy about the first trip, however, because our destination was Alabama. I had heard only negative reports about how they treated blacks there and was apprehensive about the trip. Actually I was gun-shy about the south as a whole. The trip showed me that it was safe to travel there in the 1970s, particularly if you were part of a college tennis team. I took Dad's advice about being in a group to avoid trouble and stayed close to the team, never venturing far from the tennis courts.

Dating at OSU was better for me than in high school. The exposure to black women was great, but I found it a bit discouraging. The black population in Mount Vernon was so sparse that we all seemed like family. Black women in Columbus were not overly receptive to me. Instead, they communicated, at least nonverbally, "Just who do you think you are? You're not all that special, just because you talk funny." They simply did not understand me, and I was not receptive to them because I wasn't familiar with the urban culture. It was only after repeated exposure to black girls that I was able to appreciate their distinctive beauty and feel a part of their culture. Lack of exposure had handicapped me and shut me off from my own heritage, from my roots.

One relationship was special to me during my sophomore year. I met a girl, a nice Catholic white girl. We dated on a steady basis and were looked upon as a couple. We moved among her friends and mine with relative ease as we enjoyed the usual college activities. Whether we went to a movie, attended a ball game, or simply sat on a bench on the oval and talked, we enjoyed just being with each other. We were, simply, a couple in love. Then one night it all came tumbling to the ground. We went to a floor party at her dorm where a male student started to make racial slurs directed my way. "Hey, Afro, what are you doing here with a white girl?"

My girlfriend was horrified, and my first thought was to keep this episode as non-dramatic and non-violent as possible to lessen the trauma for her. Raw hatred spurted from the mouth of this bully who outweighed me by at least seventy-five pounds. Knowing that he wasn't going to let up, I steered my girlfriend outside. He followed us, and pushed me up against a wall. I grabbed the bully and bent his thumb back until he howled with pain. He took off running. I had left my mark, and I'm sure he felt it for a long time.

One of my football buddies, who had observed this interaction, told me he had been ready to come to my aid if needed. I appreciated his watchfulness, but had suffered very little physical pain from the episode. However, my emotional pain lasted a long time because my girlfriend freaked out. She let me know that she couldn't handle the pressure attached to dating me. She ended our relationship by walking away and not looking back. Her exit left me with the foreboding forecast that my future inter-racial dating would be doomed if the girls identified me with the part of my background that was different from theirs.

After that incident, I realized that if I continued to date white girls, it would take an exceptionally strong girl with a family that was open to interracial dating. Such would be the requirement for a sustainable relationship between a white girl and me. The chances of that happening seemed bleak at the time. I wasn't resigning myself to failure, but I didn't like the idea of continually breaking new ground as situations like this might arise, and I didn't look forward to living in fear while I was dating a white girl. I was in a social dilemma that seemed to have no solution.

As I had done often in the past, I turned to reading to help me sift out this problem. I read a book which said that black men dated white women only to bring up the black man's social status. I didn't identify with this mindset because I didn't perceive that my social status was inferior either because I was black or from a small town or any other facet of my background that constituted who I was and what I was worth. I was just doing what I had been doing in a natural manner all my life: associating primarily with white people. During my childhood, elementary school, junior high, and high school white people made up my world of experiences. Why should I shift from associating with them now that I was in college? I felt more at ease with whites because of my upbringing in the small town of Mount Vernon.

My social choices were not based on class status at all. That book was not only unhelpful, it seemed absurd to me. My search for self continued as I immersed myself in tennis, an area in which I felt secure and confident.

Hitting the ball low to high in tennis not only can give you top spin, but it keeps you in control and the tennis ball in the court. If, instead of trying for winning shots on every ball you approach, you can just hit low to high and stay composed, you will keep the ball in play long enough for your opponent to make the bad shot.

Because of a strong work ethic while growing up and confidence in myself as a tennis player, I was able to do whatever it took to succeed at Ohio State and to navigate my way between worlds of black and white. By keeping the ball in play (low to high), tennis players develop perseverance and patience which can lead to more wins than losses. That was my goal in life as well as in tennis.

CHAPTER SIX

Tennis Tip: Don't let that ball drop so low; always try to catch it on the rise to clear the net better and to help you hit the ball deeper. You can misjudge the ball, or be slow to get to it, and that makes it drop too low.

My junior year at OSU turned out to be my best year in college. Lots of good fortune came my way because of tennis. My grades improved, and I was playing the best tennis of my life. It was euphoric, the feeling I imagined heaven to be like. It was the year I won the Big Ten championship. I could have stayed in that year of my life forever. It is my hope that everyone might experience a "heaven-on-earth" year. Money problems eased as I learned creative ways to get money. For example, I sold used tennis balls for a quarter apiece. It was good money, if you had a brisk business, which I did. I helped out those who wanted to save the cost of a new can of balls, so I was performing a service as well as having spending money for good times with friends. Considering today's emphasis on recycling, I was ahead of my time.

The only bad tennis match I experienced occurred at Ohio University, and it was not because of my tennis. I won the match and was walking to the van when an opposing team member, who was from India, asked me, "Did that nigger win?"

Since I was the only black member on the team, I realized he was referring to me. I asked myself "Why is this guy calling me a nigger, when he is darker than I am?" The only difference, I thought, was that he came over on a different boat! As a matter of fact, just about everyone in America arrived here on one kind of "boat" or another. All our roots are in other countries! I am glad that my teammates stopped me before I could "educate" him on these facts, and enlarge his repertoire of racial etiquette.

Since success is the best revenge, I got the last word that year by winning the Big Ten Championship at the number six slot on the team. This was a huge accomplishment for me! My record was extraordinary that year of 1978 and even the OSU paper, *The Lantern,* ran an article on me. Everything was falling into place, and I felt on top of the world! I did not let the ball drop too low.

My world got even better when I met Jenny. She was one of the greatest girls I had ever known. She was smart, good-looking, funny, wholesome, and eager to look on the positive side. Jenny accepted me unconditionally and encouraged me to be even better than I thought I could be. I took Jenny home to meet my family. Mom invited us over for Sunday dinner, and they all loved her. Jenny was also very comfortable with all of them. She talked to Valerie, who was 17 at the time, about life at Ohio State and encouraged her to apply after high school. Kiersten, who had just started high school, really looked up to this college girl and made it known that she was also headed for Ohio State. Unfortunately, Jenny couldn't meet Mark because he was off playing with some band or other. My dad was also unavailable since he now lived in Newark.

In my home there was never a problem about whom I dated – black or white. My parents always accepted every girl I dated, and never made race an issue. However, it was always a problem when I met the parents of a white girlfriend, and Jenny's parents were no different. Acceptance into the white community continued to be a hurdle. Most parents of white girls that I dated were definitely not ready to give their blessing to interracial dating, even though I am light skinned. The mantra, I believe was, "Oh, no – not with MY daughter!"

Their reactions reminded me of the concept of NIMBY (not in my back yard), where philosophical outlook bends to practical pressure. For instance, a group of people might be raising funds for a group home to help those who leave prison. However, when it comes down to the matter of where to locate the home, communities do not want former convicts in their immediate environments where they have to see them or possibly interact with them. Fear takes over. Many people fail to see the conflict between their convictions and their behavior. Parents of white girls that I tried to date may have been liberal in their thinking, but they were not totally accepting of me when reality set in that I might be a permanent fixture in their lives. This would continue to play out in my life as a young man looking for acceptance into a world in which, because of my upbringing, I thought I belonged.

A movie, *Guess Who's Coming to Dinner*, in the late 1960s caused people to think about racial mixing and inter-racial marriage as a possibility in their lives. The film provided a provocative and amusing forum in which to view the NIMBY conflict where principles and practicality collide. Starring Spencer Tracy, Katherine Hepburn, and Sidney Poitier, the film won several academy awards.

The script involves a white American woman and a man whom she is bringing home to meet her liberal, upper-class parents (Hepburn and Tracy). Her intended fiancé is Dr. Prentice (Poitier), an African American she met on vacation in Hawaii. To debunk stereotypes the writers created a young doctor who is highly intelligent, cultured, well spoken and fits in well with the upper-middle-class environment of the girl and her parents. The only conceivable barrier to his marrying the white woman would be race. No detail is left untouched as the movie shows him leaving money on a desk in the parents' home after he makes a long-distance phone call. Ultimately the girl's mother (Hepburn), who is supportive of her daughter's choice, convinces her husband, who ultimately resolves his conflict and asks: "When will dinner be served?"

Popular musicals of the day, West Side Story and *South Pacific*, were affecting the popular culture by confronting, as well as examining, bias. In the movie, *West Side Story*, Leonard Bernstein's musical (based on *Romeo and Juliet*) deals with New York City street gangs. Chita Rivera (Anita) tells Natalie Wood (Maria) to "stick to your own kind." In the film, white and Puerto Rican gangs fight each other for turf on the west side of Manhattan. The movie ends in tragedy (the Puerto

Rican girl and white boy die) because of the two groups' mutual hate and fear of people who are different. The stick-to-your- own-kind adage prevails throughout the movie. Relative to me, however, what was my own kind? If a duck has been imprinted to follow ducks, wouldn't it be unnatural for it to follow a turkey? If I had imprinted with the whites in my environment until I entered college, wouldn't it be natural that I would prefer them still? Weren't they "my own kind?" I knew no other kind. To bond with blacks because of my outward appearance and societal pressure seemed unnatural to me.

Other thought-provoking entertainment included *South Pacific.* A Rodgers and Hammerstein song, *You've Got to be Carefully Taught,* examines the roots of prejudice saying that we are taught ". . . to be afraid of people whose eyes are oddly made . . . or people whose skin is a different shade . . . you've got to be carefully taught." The song continues with: "You've got to be taught to hate and fear . . . you've got to be taught from year to year . . . it's got to drummed in your dear little ear . . . You've got to be taught before it's too late . . . before you are 6, or 7, or 8 . . . to hate all the people your relatives hate . . . you've got to be carefully taught. "

Instead of being "carefully taught" to be afraid of people who were different, my parents had taught me the opposite, to accept differences. I tried to understand the viewpoint of white parents of the girls I dated in college, but did not see myself as black or white. I was just a guy from a small town in the Midwest. Fitting in and being accepted by both whites and blacks in college continued to be a challenge with both groups. I didn't feel a need to speak in a certain way with whites and differently with blacks. I insisted on conjugating my verbs in the way I had been taught and staying true to myself.

As I began to think of a career after college, tennis was always at the front of my choices. However, I knew that the world of tennis was dominated by whites and that I would have to deal with the added pressure of my outward appearance as I mingled with the country-club set. I could see a correlation between the challenges of a tennis career that involves a dominant white culture and my ongoing challenge with parents of white girls that I dated. In both instances, I think it is always wise to withhold judgment when attempting to understand the feelings and fears of others, especially when those fears are culturally biased. As people become familiar with each other, fears often fall to the wayside.

That spring I actually got to meet Bill Cosby, a man whom I respected and who had a big influence on my world outlook. He was an avid tennis fan, and he also played tennis. I got to play tennis with him when he was in town for a short visit and called Ohio State to request someone with whom to play. I was the lucky choice. Mr. Cosby arrived in a limousine, and his driver waited while we played. Cosby was pretty good at tennis, and I definitely enjoyed hitting with him. I was determined that I would not make him look bad no matter the level of his play. We played a set that afternoon, and he was all business, no laughs or relaxing banter. I gave him a couple of games.

When the set was over, he shook my hand, got back into the limo, and away he went. In spite of his serious demeanor, I think he liked me and would have sponsored me on tour except for the fact that he was already sponsoring someone else. In hindsight, maybe I should have been more assertive about my desire to go on the tour, and let him know how important it would be for me to have him as a sponsor. However, when he called Ohio State asking for someone to play tennis with him, they told him that I was the first African-American tennis star they had had at Ohio State, so I assumed he knew my financial situation as well.

One of the best school years I ever had was followed by one of the worst summers. Jenny went back to California. My heart was broken and I felt empty without her. She had meant so much to me and eventually her parents had begun to accept me as a part of Jenny's life, but all of that ended when we were separated by an entire continent. The family had packed up and moved to California and Jenny went with them. We tried to stay in contact, but I couldn't afford the high cost of phone bills and we didn't write. We simply lost touch after awhile. No limitless cell phones or email existed then.

During the summer I continued working with the public school kids at the tennis camps held at Ohio State. Valerie came up to be with me a couple of times because she was applying to Ohio State. We had a good time together, and she enjoyed playing tennis on the Ohio State courts. I looked forward to another Ryuse attending Ohio State.

The only way my mood had to go was up, and when Coach Daly told me I would be receiving a full scholarship from the tennis program for my senior year, I made a giant step toward elation! It was not just the self-esteem boost and validation of my tennis skill that came with a full scholarship, but the financial freedom from one of the most disgusting jobs I've ever had – cleaning the OSU stadium Sunday mornings after football games. I absolutely hated that job. Life was looking up.

Misjudging people, like misjudging the tennis ball as it is dropping into your court, can lead to a lack of success in tennis and in life. Catching the ball on the rise is comparable to reaching out to others, trusting in your best judgment of others, and following through on your good instincts. To quote Shakespeare, *Julius Caesar, Act. 4*: "There is a tide in the affairs of man which, taken at the flood, leads on to fortune; we must take the current when it serves, or lose our ventures."

CHAPTER SEVEN

Tennis Tip: Start out playing high-percentage ground strokes, keeping the ball in the big part of the court as much as possible before you start going for winning shots. By keeping the ball in play for a long time, you can find your opponent's weaknesses and then go for the winning shot. This applies whether you are playing doubles or singles.

My senior year began in Baker Hall with my roommate, John Li. I was still miserable about Jenny, and knew I needed to build a life without her, but I was not hopeful that it would be possible. Then I met Elise. She lived one floor below me in the dorm, which meant that I ran into her frequently on a casual basis. One night we both went to a disco floor party and I asked her to dance. That was the beginning of a lot of fun together as a couple.

Once again, I found myself dating a Catholic white girl. The emptiness left by Jenny was slowly being filled by the happiness of being with Elise. We had a great relationship my whole senior year, and were accepted by all our friends. Everything was great until her old boyfriend heard about us and made a visit to my dorm room. He tried to persuade me that he and Elise had a love/hate relationship and that I should back off. I told him he was weird and needed to leave, but I knew that wouldn't be the end of him. Little did I know that John Li, my roommate and best friend, was in the top bunk enjoying the drama as Elise's old boyfriend and I bantered back and forth. John and I laughed about it later.

Two days later, when I was in Elise's room, the old boyfriend showed up again and grabbed her. I pushed him away from her, but he came at me and grabbed my afro. After I hit him a few times (thanks to my martial arts training), he dropped to the floor. After regaining a vertical position, he slowly backed out of the room. My physical fitness, however, was soon to be drastically compromised.

I was holding my own on the tennis team my senior year until I injured my back during a serve. The team doctor said it was a pulled muscle and gave me shots of cortisone to help the back muscles heal. The diagnosis ultimately turned out to be a fractured rib. Without that knowledge, however, I continued to play all season with the fracture. After that injury I never played up to my potential. In Indiana during a Big Ten match, I forced my body beyond its normal limits. I gave away the second set, but won the match. My opponent won more games, but that didn't win the match for him. He exemplified a true sport. He recognized the pain I had endured throughout the match. In a never-to-be-forgotten moment, he asked me to wait on the court while he ran up to his dorm to get me "a cold one" to try and numb the pain.

The disappointment of my senior year is painful, however, to this day. I had hoped that senior year would be my breakout year. Instead, I finished the year with a disappointing record. I was thankful to have Elise by my side because she continued to be supportive during this time in my career.

I wrapped up my college career in tennis and finished my degree in Recreation Education at OSU. Mom, Dad, Valerie, Mark, and Kiersten came for the graduation ceremony which was held in Ohio Stadium. Several of the Beatty Park tennis friends were also there which made me happy. Afterward we had a great meal at the Jai Lai which was a popular restaurant not too far from the stadium. My dad, especially, was bursting with pride at seeing the first member of his family graduate from college. They were hoping that Valerie, who recently was graduated from high school and planning to enter OSU in the fall, would be the second Ohio State graduate in the family.

Even Mark seemed pleased, but I felt bad for him. He had several girlfriends at the time, but no real goals or opportunities. At that time he was working as a cook in Mount Vernon at the one, big restaurant in town. My girlfriend, Elise, was celebrating with her family so we didn't spend any time together on graduation day. She made a quick appearance to say hello to my family, but had to return to her own.

Graduation Day from The Ohio State University

Once we had graduated, Elise moved back to northern Ohio, and I stayed in Columbus. We could see each other only in Columbus because her parents did not know we were still dating. When she visited, she began to seem distant. I asked her if she thought we were still a couple. She assured me that we were, but it became apparent she was having a hard time handling her exclusively white world at home and our black-white world in Columbus. I loved her dearly and understood it was not easy for her, but it left me feeling once again that my relationships with white women were doomed. Elise and I broke up and she eventually married a white man.

After leaving college behind in 1978, I was determined to pursue a career as a professional tennis instructor, a club pro. At Ohio State I had learned an incredible lot from the coaches and my teammates. I left there with my initial passion for tennis intact as well as an even greater respect for the game. I knew that I would achieve ongoing satisfaction in my tennis career. My education at Ohio State was meaningful, rewarding, and fun. Those three ingredients were the imperative goals that I was determined to include in my lifelong work with tennis students. I was eager to begin my career as a pro.

My first choice of a tennis club in which I'd like to work didn't pan out. Maybe I was naïve, but I was genuinely surprised when one of my previous tennis coaches told me that he had overheard one of the owners say that he did not want a lot of "jungle bunnies" hanging out there. Obviously, that place would not be a good fit for me, so my search continued. I interviewed with another club, Olympic Tennis Club, and was hired right away to teach tennis. It wasn't long before I started to earn a good salary and to make a name for myself in the tennis community.

My dad had two reasons to visit Columbus now. He frequently came to the Olympic Tennis Club to see me at work teaching tennis. Then he would also visit Valerie who was at Ohio State, but homesick from the start. No matter how often both parents visited her, and in spite of the fact that I was nearby and tried to see her as much as I could during my busy first year at Olympic, Ohio State didn't work out for her. She just couldn't adjust to the size of it. Finally she dropped out and returned to Mount Vernon. Mom helped her get into Mount Vernon Nazarene College which suited her better. She began a career in computer technology.. It seemed that Valerie had a promising career because computer science was in its infancy at the time, with jobs readily available to those who possessed skills in that area.

Right from the start, feedback from students assured me that I was making a difference in their lives. I still tell my tennis students that the most important outcome of the game is to have fun and enjoy the sport. I have always tried to make my instruction fun for them. Whether students are young or old, they learn best when they are having fun and being encouraged as they grow in their skills. One of my ways of making instruction fun continues to be fantasy tournaments. At the end of a "Play-and-Learn" session, I promise the winners a week in the Bahamas (when it is ten-below-zero in Columbus). With guys, especially, I'll throw in a fancy convertible that they'll be driving when they win. The fantasy is fun and relaxing. Students play a lot better when they are motivated even with a make-believe prize.

On a more serious note, whether my students are age 5 or 85, I ask them to set goals for themselves, and then to note their improvement. However, tennis players must love the game to continue to be the best they can be. A few of my colleagues and I have students who have stayed with us for twenty years and more because they have developed a passion for the sport and realize that the "pros" share that passion. Tennis tips are compatible with tips for successful living as a whole.

At the time I began my career, there were very few black members at Olympic Tennis Club. Still, it felt comfortable for me and I felt accepted because I had been around white people, starting with my small-town roots, and it really didn't bother me. Arthur Ashe, my role model, helped open the doors into the tennis world, especially the country club doors, for black tennis pros like me. I think that, because of his accomplishments in tennis and my own ease around white people, I was well accepted at Olympic. Even though Arthur Ashe retired in 1980 as a competitive player, he was still announcing games and furthering the positive image of tennis in any way he could.

I had been working at Olympic for three years, and the work was going well until my father passed away in 1981. He was employed at the Heath Air Force Base until the day he died. After his cancer was diagnosed in 1975, he was determined to face it head-on and not let it slow him down. Due to that determination, he continued working at Heath beyond most doctors' predictions. I felt that his desire to see me develop as a tennis player and establish a career in tennis kept him going. He hung on to life for an incredibly long time.

Mom and he had remained in touch, and my mother got along with his new wife. My parents had divorced in 1973 after years of ups and downs in their married life. Unlike a lot of parents who divorce, they never tried to get the kids to take sides. Mark, Kiersten,

Valerie and I went to his house for Christmas four days before he died. Everyone tried to stay upbeat, but we all knew Dad didn't have much time left. He died during the night on December 29, 1981, at his house. I don't suppose anyone is ever ready to let a loved one go, and I most certainly was not. I took his death very hard. This was my first experience losing someone close to me. He was my dad, my coach, and my friend. I felt his love and his pride in me as well as a physical closeness no matter how great the actual distance between us. I felt lost and abandoned without him in my life.

His funeral was held in Newark, and he was buried in a turtleneck sweater at his request. He had also requested to wear a medallion that had belonged to Mom. On that dreary gray day, as I drove from Columbus to my father's funeral, it was hard to keep the tears from falling so that I could drive. Mom explained to me that Mark couldn't be there because he was playing in a band outside Ohio and needed the income. She said Mark cried a little bit during their phone conversation. I know that Mark had to feel awful about Dad's death even if they had been distant because of all the arguments resulting from the way Mark had handled his life. Dad never got over the fact that Mark, who had so much talent and possessed so many gifts, ended up basically a failure according to the way that Dad measured success. To Dad's way of thinking, Mark had been given benefits that he as a boy never had; and Dad never totally understood the mental illness that interfered with Mark's success. A few of the old crowd from Beatty Park showed up at the funeral, and that was nice.

Around the time of Dad's death, Valerie was dating a guy in Columbus and considering moving into a serious relationship with him. Mom knew about it, but was strongly advising her against it. Kiersten was a high school senior. Mom had gotten a great job at Cooper Energy, a good career change after the job with F.H.A. She worked as a teletype operator and was involved in correspondence in Kuwait and other faraway places. Her job was exciting to her, and she had a lot of responsibility for inventory control which was basic to the company. I was glad that she had also become socially active in the decade since their divorce.

For me, though, things were going to become even bleaker. In the following year, after Dad's funeral, I suffered another back injury and was not able to work for most of the summer. My dad's death and my injury led to a very tough and depressing summer. The doctors thought my back spasms might be a result of mental stress caused by my father's death. I started playing tennis again with my sister, Kiersten, who was visiting me prior to the fall when she would be in a dorm at Ohio

State. She and I became best buddies and enjoyed each other's company thoroughly. Every Friday we'd go out for a large pizza with all the toppings. She was a high-energy young woman who could afford the calories, especially since she played so much tennis. I was helping her get ready for the Ohio State team, and could feed her balls and offer corrective advice; however, due to my back injury I couldn't burn up the calories as she could. My weight wasn't good, but it wasn't too out of control. My chief problem was that I was "self-medicating" by drinking shots of tequila to numb the back pain. When my back loosened up, I gave up the tequila and returned to work in 1982.

When I returned to work at Olympic, I was living in my second apartment with friends from Baker Hall, which had been my campus dormitory. My main recreation after work was to go out with them to dance at clubs in order to meet people, mainly girls. I was "keeping the ball in play until I could find a winning shot." However, as month turned to month, I found no one who could replace Elise.

The tide turned, however, in the winter of 1982, when I ran into Lana and her friend, Laurie, at Jericho's, which was located at the Continent, a fashionable meeting place for singles on the north side of Columbus. Lana was married at the time, but Laurie and I became dancing buddies and then started dating. The fun stopped when Laurie's mother found out about us and wanted her to date a white guy from work. Laurie ended up dating both of us awhile until I found out. That didn't work for me, so we broke up, and I actually started dating my first black girl, Monique. Monique was my sister Kiersten's roommate at Ohio State. Now, that was a switch, dating a black girl. Meeting her parents for the first time was fun and a relief because they didn't have any problem with me.

Unfortunately, Monique was eight years younger than I, and we were in different phases of our lives. It was a short-lived romance which helped me sort out some of my ideas about dating. I began to realize that I, too, suffered from racial prejudice, and it was against my own race. I had been focusing on the differences, rather than the similarities, between white women and women of color. In assigning race such a high priority, I had lost sight of the fact that race is only one part of a woman's (or man's) totality. My new outlook gave me courage to start dating women of all races. That understanding broadened my thinking and opened my world to a greater degree.

I ran into Lana a year later and discovered that she was now divorced. Lana and I started to date, and she introduced me to her parents. I could not believe their reaction! This was the first time I had ever met white parents who were accepting of me. Their only problem was that they felt like she was rushing into another relationship too soon after her divorce. That took care of that. Lana listened to her parents, and our relationship ended before it could have a fair chance at success.

Lana shared with me that she had divorced because her first husband was abusive. We had strong feelings for each other, but decided to spend some time apart. We continued our friendship but didn't date. She eventually married a dentist which is what her dad was hoping she would do. She wound up emulating friends who lived next door to her. The guy was a dentist, and his wife was a nurse. In fact, that couple introduced Lana to the dentist whom she eventually married. It was interesting, too, that she went back to school and became a nurse. Lana may have been looking for a different lifestyle than I could have provided for her. She became the nurse, but I was not about to become the dentist.

After Lana and I broke up, I buried myself in work. I became even more ambitious in trying to establish myself in the tennis community in Columbus. With so much work, my social life was too limited to scope out black girls. Because I was weary of rejection from white girls, and I found no black girls on the tennis courts where I spent most of my waking hours, dating ceased for me for awhile.

My sister, Valerie, at this time had met and fallen in love with a man who lived in Hilliard. They began an affair which was to last for sixteen years. During the time she lived with the guy, she worked at CompuServe and was building a career in the software industry. She had definitely found her career choice. It was good to have her relatively nearby, and they had me over now and then. It seemed odd at the time that he tried to match me in purchases like sports cars and big-screen televisions. It was almost as if he was competing to be the "big guy" for Valerie. I liked nothing about him, but put up with him for my sister's sake. I'd have our whole family to my place for barbecues and family traditional dinners like Thanksgiving. This was easier than driving back and forth to Mount Vernon. Occasionally Kirsten and Ross were able to join us at my house before they started their family.

Mark, unfortunately, was having a bad time with his mental illness. He was admitted as a patient in the Columbus Psychiatric Hospital, which formerly had been called the Columbus State Hospital for the Insane on the west side of Columbus. He was in and out of that facility for three or four years. He would come home to

Mount Vernon and visit Mom occasionally, but I didn't see him a lot. He came around the tennis club once in a while to borrow money.

His art was an index to the disturbing state of his mind. When Mom showed me some sketches that he did while visiting her in Mount Vernon during this period, the scenes were not at all tranquil as his water colors had been earlier in his life. Instead, they depicted violence and morbidity with stark, bold colors and contrasts. The feeling projected from the art was uncontrolled aggression. Looking at the art was a jolt because I sensed a degree of madness at the center. This undoubtedly was a window into his mind at the time and perhaps a foreshadowing of future events.

My tennis world was enjoyable and rewarding. By 1986, I had developed one of the most successful junior programs in the city. I was still playing competitive tennis and won the city championships in doubles (two men vs. two men) and mixed doubles (male and female partnerships) in the late '80s. As time went on, however, the possibility of personal injury prevented me from playing because I could not afford to miss a paycheck.

I was playing at Wolfe Park on the east side of the city, because this was where most of the championships were held. This park was also a favorite place for blacks to play tennis, and I had been familiar with it since my childhood. One day I was playing there and caught the eye of a pretty black woman named Annette. She started taking lessons from me; and, after a while, I stopped charging her for lessons as we began dating. Around this time Steffi Graf, who had one of the best slice backhands I've ever seen in a men's or women's game, had been awarded the Golden Slam/Grand Slam in Singles.

Annette, as well as women tennis players across the country, was thrilled because that award meant that Steffi had won Wimbledon, the French Open, Australian Open and U.S. Open. Additionally she had won an Olympic gold medal for tennis. That's why "Golden Slam" became part of the title. Steffie was the only tennis star to have accomplished that, which impressed Annette, as it did thousands of young women who became interested in learning to play the game. Tennis became the rage for women because of champions like Steffi and Monica Seles.

People in the black tennis community began talking about my dating a black girl and teased me about it, but it was clear that they approved. Even though not one of them had ever mentioned it to me, I discovered that it had bothered them that I had dated white girls exclusively. I knew that some of them had a problem with that. When Annette approached me about that, I had to admit it was true, but only because I was rarely around black women! As it turned out, my relationship with Annette was short lived because tennis was the only glue that bound our relationship. I couldn't take it, because she wanted to play tennis constantly, even on Saturday nights. Traditionally, that was a night I needed for relaxation, anything but tennis. After being on tennis courts all day, I just didn't want to play any more tennis. We simply didn't have a sufficient number of common interests to keep us together. A positive side-effect of that relationship, however, was that I became more confident about dating women of any race.

Tennis was thriving during this period, not only because of the stellar women players that Annette and my sisters were in awe of, but also players like Andre Agassi and Pete Sampras. Agassi burst onto the scene in 1986 and prided himself as a non-conformist player as far as what he wore on the court. His wild hair and crazy clothes took the prize for non conventional court appearance. Agassi was from the new school of tennis and liked playing on the base line: staying far back and hitting with power. His strong and fast ground-stroke game was exciting. His style – not only of dress but technique – differed markedly from Pete Sampras who favored an old school style of serve and volley. It was fun to watch Sampras and Agassi play because the contrast made for an exciting match. Agassi, who turned pro at age 16, was perhaps the best return-of-serve player ever. Like Steffi Graf, he also won the Golden Slam/Grand Slam.

It was clear that none of the Ryuse kids was going on the pro tour, no matter how much we liked tennis or how we performed on Ohio State's tennis teams. Kiersten, our last Ohio State tennis player, was now getting ready to graduate and leave tennis behind her for awhile. Being a business graduate, she was ready to move on and start making a name for herself in the business world. She took a job at Macy's in Atlanta. She worked there for a year before accepting a sales representative job in New Orleans where she met the man who was going to change her life.

Kiersten playing tennis at O.S.U.

She met Ross in New Orleans where they were successful sales representatives for competing companies. Ross worked for Nabisco, and Kiersten worked for Quaker Oats. They engaged in a friendly competition over display space in supermarkets. Both of them lived in the same trendy apartment complex which was geared toward the yuppie generation. This was typical of the upwardly mobile young professional in the late 1980s. The fact that Ross was white was not an issue with either family. Our whole family liked Ross from the start, and Kiersten was as open as I was in regard to people outside her race.

Ross, being the correct gentleman, called my mother to ask for Kiersten's hand in marriage. After Mom's approval, he took her to a romantic setting, Bermuda, to propose to her. His family lived in Wisconsin where his father was a "favorite son" of their community. Ross had attended the University of Illinois and played baseball. I have to admit that being athletic was an asset in our family. Mom got busy with wedding plans, and our two families came together to celebrate their wedding at Ascension Lutheran Church in Columbus. I gave her away. Mark was an usher, and Valerie was the maid of honor.

Both Kiersten and I had kept the ball in play long enough to make a winning shot as far as our careers were concerned. Our family felt that Ross definitely was a winner, and we were glad that Kiersten and I had both persevered in order to attain diplomas at Ohio State. Every shot doesn't have to be a winner; you need patience in order to wait for the winning shot to come. I was still looking for a winner in the romance area, as my sister had already won the point for that.

CHAPTER EIGHT

Tennis Tip: The worst mistake in tennis is hitting the ball into the net. To lessen this problem, keep high clearance of the ball over the net in a cross-court pattern.

The wedding of Kiersten and Ross brought light to an otherwise dark period in the life of the Ryuse family. Mark's condition was quickly sliding down a fast slope. He was now living in a halfway house, called Belvedere, which was located near the psychiatric hospital on the west side of Columbus, just west of downtown. He was not coming around me much, and Mom was not seeing much of him either. Because of that, she was even more scared and worried than before. She would drink and pretend everything was all right, yet it was not. She knew that he was associating with some strange people, including drug dealers and homeless people who were down on their luck and mentally unstable. A few times her phone rang, and she was startled by strange voices that made no sense.

Mark would speak about women in his life from time to time, but he had no foundation to even begin to think of building a relationship with a rational woman. Mom knew that he was continuing to play drums at one particular east side bar which worried her because it was in such a rough neighborhood. Mom visited there at least once, and was literally scared for her life. She wasn't sleeping well, was drinking too much, and had all the signs of alcoholism. Even though I was concerned about Mom, I left a lot of her care to my sister, Valerie. I learned later that Valerie went through a lot of pain with Mom and her troubles at that time, yet she kept it to herself. I justified the fact that I was shifting a lot of responsibility to Valerie by telling myself that it was probably easier for Mom to tell her troubles to a daughter than a son.

In the early 1990s, work was changing due to the growth of tennis facilities in Columbus. Tennis clubs were being built in the suburbs, and some of my students were joining the new clubs out of convenience. Withstanding this loss, I still had a good business and was able to buy my first condominium. I had a roommate, Joe, who was from the inner city of Columbus. Even though he was white, he was more black oriented than I because of the environment into which he was born. Joe was raised in the kind of environment with which most people would assume I was familiar. If people looked at the two of us and made judgments about who was "black" based on skin-color, their assessments would be the opposite of reality. Joe had grown up surrounded by blacks and knew far more about black culture than I did. It is amusing and ironic that we were the complete opposite of each other in that respect.

Joe was so much more relaxed around black people than I was. In a fashion sense, his clothes, hats and shoes were more similar to those you would see in the inner city. The way he walked and talked resonated more with blacks. When Joe saw me dancing for the first time, he laughed at me. I still remember his surprise. "Loosen up, man! Let me show you some moves." I learned about myself through Joe and miss his friendship now that he lives in Houston. Joe's lifestyle and outlook only confirms my thoughts about imprinting and its influence on behavior.

I did not date much during this time, but I had a good friend named Lacey, who was white. We had a lot in common because she was athletic. Lacey owned her own gym and taught gymnastics. She was interested in tennis and especially liked Monica Seles who was the youngest-ever French Open champion in 1990 when she was only sixteen years old. Mary Corello said of Monica's achievement: "This is the age of Big Babe tennis." Lacey admired Monica Seles as a tennis player who worked out to obtain a high degree of physical fitness which took her game (and tennis) to a new level. Lacey and I have remained friends for several years. Lacey helped me through some tough times, especially during the troubled years of my brother's illness and financial problems that accompanied that period of his life. My mother was fond of Lacey and pleased that she was concerned about our family at that time. Little did I know that just around the corner a tragedy was about to strike my family, a tragedy that would forever change us.

On a bitterly cold winter night in February of 1991, my brother, Mark, called me. He was frantic. He kept repeating, "They took my car! They took my car! They took my car!" I could tell he was off his medication for schizophrenia because he wasn't making any sense. Then the phone line went dead. I immediately called my mother, and she said she had received the same type of call from Mark. The next morning, Mom and I went to look for him at the halfway house where he lived, but he was nowhere to be found. We called the police who found no evidence of foul play. There was nowhere else to check except the bar where he played the drums in a band. The bar's manager said he had come by to pick up his check a week before, and they had not heard from him since.

The last time I saw Mark (before the night of the hysterical phone call) was in December of 1990, when he came to Olympic to borrow money from me. Because the look on his face was so bizarre when he entered Olympic Tennis, the manager knew that Mark was in his own world. It was helpful that the manager had seen Mark before at the tennis club and knew about his mental problems. It also helped that the manager had been active in tennis tournaments when Mark and I were playing on the tennis circuit in high school and college and was sympathetic to Mark's problems. I was in the middle of a lesson when my manager approached the court where I was working. I suspected by his facial expression and hurried walk that something shocking had occurred. He told me that I needed to go talk with my brother right away, and he offered to take my class so that I could leave immediately.

I took Mark out to my car where we sat and talked. He had wrecked his Mustang the previous night, and admitted that the wreck was his fault. Under the influence of drugs or alcohol, maybe both, he had smashed it into a guardrail. He wasn't physically injured by the crash; instead, he had walked away from the accident. He said he had called Mom to come and pick him up. However, this is the crazy part. Mark assured me that repairing the car would be no problem at all. "I can re-assemble the car to its perfect condition by using my mental powers." When I expressed skepticism about how that could be done, he was adamant about convincing me that he possessed the mental force to reconstruct, through thought, a mass of matter and restore the car to its perfect condition.

At that point weariness and exasperation got the better part of me. I simply didn't know what to say to Mark or what to do. I used the excuse that I had to get back on the court as a way to escape further efforts to deal with his situation. It is true that I had back-to-back lessons and clinics booked for the rest of the day, but a family emergency was occurring, and I should have stayed with him. Instead, I jerked a couple of twenties out of my pocket, and Mark quickly stuffed them into his jeans. Mark knew he was being dismissed. We said good-by, and he got out of the car.

As Mark turned to walk across the parking lot at Olympic Tennis Club, I noticed how his frayed denim jacket flapped in the cold December wind against his thin body. The wind appeared strong enough to lift him up and blow him away. His slight frame began to disappear from my view as he walked between the cars in the lot and headed south on the sidewalk. I had a lump in my throat, and for a second I felt a terrible urge to chase after him, to try and turn him around and away from whatever was controlling him. He was only a shadow of the brother I had known. I assumed that he had a ride waiting, or he might have been riding the city bus back to his halfway house. Instead of running after him, though, I kept to my schedule and hurried back inside to teach my waiting students.

That afternoon was the last time I would see my brother alive. Less than two months later, after that terrible phone call, Mark was missing for an entire year. For a solid year we worried every single day about his fate and didn't know if he was dead or alive. Every phone call put us on instant alert. To this day we do not know what happened to Mark after the phone line went dead on that dreadful February night of 1991.

In tennis terminology, I had definitely "hit into the net" that December day when I did not keep Mark there with me and seek help for him at that moment in time. Regret is a bitter pill. Even today it is hard to let go of "what if's" and to reconcile myself to the impossible task of controlling another person no matter how much you love that person.

During that terrible year of stress and worry about her son, my mother sank into a deep depression. Although she had been developing a drinking problem for some time before that last telephone call from Mark, she succumbed totally to alcohol now to deal with her pain and to cope with the guilt and grief surrounding Mark's disappearance. She had no reason for guilt, but parents assume it when something goes wrong for their children. Someone once said that parents take too much credit and too much blame for how their kids turn out. I certainly agree with that. Everyone but Mom could see that she had nothing to feel guilty about because she had spent countless hours of effort and much of her hard-earned money to help Mark for most of his adult life. Mom began her own descent after this horrible, year-long period of fear and uncertainty surrounding the life of her first-born son. Alcohol, unfortunately, became her refuge and opened the door to her cave of escape.

Valerie let me know then the extent to which Mom had been drinking even before Mark's disappearance. When she lived with Mom in Mount Vernon, Valerie kept the volume of Mom's alcohol consumption from me. "Mom was constantly looking for drinking buddies," she stated, and then went on to say that shortly after Dad's funeral, Mom went out for drinks with Dad's wife. That marked a kind of desperation that was shocking to me. I became alarmed that Mom might be heading in the same dangerous direction as Mark and feared for her life. I knew for sure that Dad was dead and that Mark was feared dead. Now, it appeared that Mom was on the brink of disaster. Something had to be done right away.

When I broached the subject with her, Mom claimed that Valerie was exaggerating and that she had everything under control. Alcoholics are smooth when they want to convince you against your better judgment. I bought her argument for the most part, but I started looking for signs of addiction after that conversation with Valerie. I discovered one shortly afterward on Thanksgiving. As she was getting the turkey ready to go into the oven in the early morning hours, Mom was drinking Jack Daniels. Before anyone else was up and hours before breakfast, she was basting the turkey with one hand and sneaking drinks with the other. By dinner time, she was too plastered to speak clearly or walk without staggering.

To make matters worse, Mom's job with Cooper would be changing during this tumultuous time. Their corporate office was in Houston, but Mount Vernon was the second largest office. At that time Mom had been offered a choice of going to another office out of state (possibly Houston) or taking a different position locally. She chose to leave Cooper. That decision should have alerted me but it went undetected as a clue to her condition. I thought she was just too attached to leave her hometown, but she was giving up a retirement plan and years invested in a meaningful career. Mom was much too consumed by her passion for alcohol to deal logically with a career decision that would affect the rest of her working life.

After giving up her job, drinking completely took over! Not only was her son presumed dead, but now she had no job. Her life was reeling out of control like a runaway train that she couldn't catch. She was drunk more often than she was sober, and it was easier for her to hide her drinking from us because she was living in Mount Vernon by herself. Valerie, who had been a witness to some of the ugliest scenes as the addiction was making its claim on Mom's life, had left Mount Vernon.

Mom admits that she was highly creative in concealing her behavior for the past ten years at least, as most alcoholics can be. She hid her "stash" and fooled most of us for a long time. Submitting completely to the snares of alcoholism, she not only neglected caring for herself, but quit caring about everything around her, including the house in which she had lived and spent her best years caring for her family. When the bank threatened to foreclose, she sold the house for whatever they would give her. Many significant attachments to Mount Vernon were swept away as if caught in a flash flood when she lost the house and all her furniture. She sold whatever she could for whatever money she could get to support her alcoholism. When she was broke, I let her move in with me in Columbus. She had lost it all, but she still didn't realize her desperation. She continued to drink and continued to hide it from me.

When she moved into my condominium, she was able to hold temporary jobs in Columbus until 1992. When they at last found a skull in the Scioto River, police detectives had the means to identify the missing Mark Ryuse. The skull was the last of Mark's body parts that had been found. Divers brought up parts of his body, a little at a time during that year of disappearance. At first they found a tennis shoe, then later a leg, an arm, then a torso. It was only after they had found his skull that they were able to determine his identification from dental records. Fortunately Mom was with me when she received the call telling her that Mark's body was identified.

The night when the coroner determined they had found Mark, the police telephoned my residence and asked for Mom. She was in the kitchen of my condo. I have always been thankful that I was there with her when she received the call, and the coroner confirmed her worst fear. I thought to myself, "At least, now she knows where he is." The authorities never found any clues to determine how he died. Did thugs throw him into the river? Did he jump from the Broad Street bridge? What exactly happened? I always suspected he was killed by drug dealers, but we just don't know.

An amazing outpouring of love and admiration from the Beatty Park tennis players in Columbus was uplifting to us at Mark's funeral. It was held at the Methodist church in Mount Vernon where in past years my grandmother had played the piano and organ. My sisters did not take Mark's death as hard as my mother and I did because they had steeled themselves to expect the worst based on his past downward spiral.

Valerie had admired Mark when she was a young teen and he was in high school. Mom told us that Valerie had sobbed hard when Mark left home for school at Kent State. However, in the intervening years, Valerie had grown a tough skin regarding Mark after seeing how painful his behavior had been for Mom. More than any of us, Valerie understood Mom and her trials and tribulations with Mark. Valerie was, accordingly, more concerned for Mom than Mark during those troubled days and nights when the police in Mount Vernon were regular visitors at Mom's door. Nevertheless, Valerie was upset at the loss of her older brother.

Kiersten's behavior surprised all of us because she gave off an attitude of: "What else could you expect?"

I'm sure she cared; but, because of the age difference between her and Mark and the stress he had caused for the family, her reaction to his death appeared cold. She had only heard about and seen the bad elements associated with Mark. As the baby of the family, she was only in grade school when he went off to college. As a result, Kiersten had witnessed very few of Mark's good traits. We never saw her cry, which doesn't mean that she didn't. However, her tough façade and apparent lack of feeling made the rest of us even sadder. Ross was there providing the solace lacking from his wife. Even though he had known only the "crazy" Mark, he knew there had been better times in Mark's life and was hurt by the tragic loss of a man in his prime.

As for me, I was experiencing both grief and anger. In looking back, I was angry at Mark, angry at God perhaps, but most of all angry at myself for not being able to help him with the mental illness which resulted in his death. Grief like that never goes away. It simply recedes for awhile as we conduct our daily lives, but reappears when we least expect it. A piece of music on the radio can bring back the pain of losing my brother. My heart still aches when I think of Mark and the times we were close before his illness took him away. When I see two young brothers playing tennis – and one perhaps teasing the other – I am reminded of Mark and me. I am thankful that Dad was not here to suffer the loss with us when Mark disappeared and his body was found.

Dad's presence was felt, however, when we looked around us at the church and found many of his friends from Columbus. Much to our surprise and delight, the tennis players from Beatty Park traveled to Mount Vernon to the memorial. These were some of the first black professionals with whom Mark and I interacted as kids. Dickie James, Jim Spivey, Bill Harris, Lee Townsel, and Stan Dickson had been wonderful mentors to Mark and me. These men were extra special to me because they helped Mark and me when Dad would take us to Beatty Park when we were young and upcoming tennis players and supported me after I entered Ohio State and became a Columbus resident.

When I first came to Ohio State, I was able to continue playing the style of tennis that I had learned from them in an atmosphere of camaraderie and warmth reminiscent of my dad's instruction. The tennis at Beatty Park and Wolfe Park during the time of my adolescence was different than one would find at a tennis club or country club today. In fact, the Beatty Park group created their own sort of "country club" without the pretention. There were no membership forms or fees, no dress codes, no hidden agendas. Similar to clubs, though, the players made connections.

After I left college and established a career in tennis, I could appreciate even to a greater degree their early influence and what they had meant to all of us. Living in Columbus, it would have been easy for me to stay in touch, but my hectic life got in the way and I had not taken the time to stay in touch with them on a regular basis. Now they became even more special after Dad's and Mark's deaths because their presence offered a connection to my dad and brother that I could find nowhere else.

Although the "membership" at Beatty had been overwhelmingly black, whites were also welcome and included. Jake Slosser and Frank Barnett are two names that stand out. Frank was 31 when he first started playing tennis, and by the time he met my dad, Mark and me, he was 36 and had won 5 big tournaments, including participation at the U.S. Open. Frank Barnett is still an active player at the age of seventy-eight. When I spoke with him recently, we talked about the "good old days" and he reminded me that: "Your dad was always watching out for his boys."

In that same conversation, Frank talked about how the black players at Beatty would egg each other on, being strong competitors who made each other better. It was not just about proving who was best, although they did have informal tournaments. More importantly, though, everyone knew and respected the talent of everyone else. That special group – mainly but not exclusively black - were more interested in having fun than in the competitive aspect of play. Frank said he always thought I was a highly intense player (in part, perhaps, to curry approval from Dad and Mark), and added that I may have gone farther if I had been able to loosen up more and to enjoy the game more. It is possible that I could have enjoyed those games more had I not been so intense; however, I was able to challenge my elders as well as learn from them. I smiled to myself as I remembered a 13-year-old holding my own in a game of tennis with Frank and the others there.

No one influenced my game or instructed me as effectively as my dad, but my experiences with these strong and supportive men as I was growing up reminded me of the African proverb, later used by Hillary Clinton, that "It takes a village to raise a child." Beatty Park was my "village." Their support and presence during this difficult time demonstrated how tightly knit the black community was at Beatty Park and made me aware of my isolation from this kind of community during my growing up in Mount Vernon. They have continued to support and advise me during my tennis career as a junior instructor and teaching pro. I have always appreciated the white professional men as well, who could have been club members elsewhere but chose to play at Beatty and Wolfe instead. Sadly they remember Mark as being "off the deep end" much of the time. At any rate their presence at Mark's funeral was wonderful.

Now was the time for Mom to start getting the help she needed, but it wasn't easy getting her to accept help. We knew that her depression was a combined result of Mark's disappearance and her job loss. However, we attributed the most significant reason for her depression to alcohol abuse. For a good while, I was either in denial or deliberately chose to overlook Mom's problem with alcohol. It didn't take me long, however, to catch on after she moved in with me because she was drunk more often than sober. After I finally realized I could not deal with her alcoholic behavior, and that living with me was not helping her, I kicked her out of my house. That was not easy, but I knew that I wasn't helping her. In fact, I would be enabling her if conditions remained the same.

After she left my house, she lived with Valerie, who was the "good cop," opposed to me as the "bad cop." Valerie and her significant other eventually realized that they were enabling her as I had been. At Valerie's suggestion, Mom entered Riverside Hospital's program for alcoholics. However, it was little help because Mom's disease was more advanced than their program at that time. Living with Valerie, however, was not an option, so Mom went to live with two of her best friends after Valerie asked her to leave.

Her two friends couldn't provide any more help than Valerie and I had. One of the two friends convinced her to seek help at Maryhaven. Real, effective treatment was to begin there. After she had been there for 28 days, Maryhaven required a six-month residency in the women's program. Mom was totally ready to be cured and signed herself up. She came to realize that there was no shame in admitting she was an alcoholic and needed help. The only shame she felt was remorse for the awful things she had done while under the influence, including drunken driving on several occasions.

At Maryhaven, she discovered that alcoholism affects men and women across all ethnic and economic groups. She remembered that the former first lady, Betty Ford, had sought treatment. Mom also found that group therapy was truly an equalizer. It takes an alcoholic to see through the tricks and schemes of another one. People from all walks of life realize that they have a common problem and they have all sunk to depths where they never would have believed they could go. Mom got back her life through the treatment.

When she became sober, she talked with all of us freely about her disease. Her addiction to alcohol had been building up for a long time, she said. It had filled a need that she had for peace, just as it has for millions. She opened up and told us about all the unusual places where she had hidden her stash of alcohol and about the times she had driven her car while she was drunk. We were thankful that she was still alive, and amazed at how effectively (and creatively) she had fooled us and for how long she had lived this charade. She told us about many scary adventures she had under the influence of alcohol as she was living by herself in Mount Vernon after her kids had moved on and established different lives. All had left but Mark. Mark had been the mainstay in her life whom she was constantly bailing out of jail and worrying about day after day, night after night. Her only comfort had come from a bottle.

She told us that she could no longer hide her alcoholism from us after Mark disappeared. Maybe she just didn't have the energy to hide it any longer. It wasn't until after his memorial service, however, that she realized she needed help. When she decided to get help for herself, she assumed for herself the optimism she had always had for others. She became a faithful member of Alcoholics Anonymous and is still sober today. I am proud of Mom for her victory over that vicious disease. Her presence is delightful, and she is always optimistic and uplifting to us. Highly energetic, she still has a bounce to her step and a twinkle in her eye.

Throughout Mark's disappearance and subsequent death, I buried myself in my work. The rougher my private life was, the harder I worked as I took over the summer program at Olympic Tennis Club. Everything was going well, but it was clear to me that I needed to delegate some of the day-to-day organization to one of the pros. There was a general buzz among the pros about which one of them would be selected for the position; and, to prevent divisiveness among them, I decided to place the solitary woman pro in charge. She had equal qualifications; and, in my opinion, could do the job as well as any of the men. She would communicate with the pros and students about assignments of students to specific tennis clinics. Additionally, she would ask the pros for input.

My decision started a series of events that took years to resolve. As soon as my choice was announced, one of the pros, a male Muslim, was incensed by it. He was insulted by the notion of a woman having authority over him. For him this was a serious, cultural-born issue. In front of several students and others, he called me a "ni' ger." I was stunned, partly because his skin color was much darker than mine. However, I kept my cool and replied, "If you're going to call me that, at least **pronounce** the insult correctly! The word is pronounced "nig' ger" not "ni' ger."

After recognizing his insult and replying as I did, I was ready to move on, but he would simply not let it go. He lunged at me, swinging and hurling a tennis racket, and I knew it was going to be tough resolving the situation. My goal was to get him out of my face and try to pin him to the ground. I yelled for someone to call the police. I was defending myself the best I could, being always aware that my job depended on my body being in one piece and strong.

He had been around long enough to know that I had suffered a bad leg injury recently. It was clear that his goal was to attack my bad leg with his racket. He clobbered me pretty well, but I got a few self-defense shots in with my racket, basically trying to knock his racket out of his hand. One whack of my racket landed on his left shoulder. If I had been trying to beat him up, it would have been easy to do as I was in much better shape at the time. That was not my goal, however. I just wanted the incident to come to an end as we were attracting a crowd. Eventually the police came and removed him from the tennis courts.

Shortly after the incident, he contacted the tennis club and presented me with magnified photos of his injuries and sued me for "over defending" myself. Even though I was in the right – and had several witnesses to prove it – this episode did not bode well for my career. Simply put, there was no way this was going to help the image of a black pro working with mostly white tennis students in a country-club setting.

This altercation heightened my awareness of differences in people's cultures and beliefs, and I began to more completely understand cultural sensitivity. During the conflict with the Muslim who had gender issues about a woman being an authority figure, I definitely "kept the ball in play and did not hit into the net." Because I was able to keep my cool as much as possible while defending my body from injury, my ball had "high clearance" and I was hitting "cross-court." However, another version of "court" was soon to result from this troublesome incident.

CHAPTER NINE

Tennis Tip: The Toss. The toss is the beginning and ending of your serve. You can't create a good form to deliver the right shot unless your toss is correct. Before you change anything about your serve, look at your toss first.

Cultural sensitivity is not limited to people from other countries, such as the Muslim who had attacked me, but applies to the cultural environment of our country as well. I heard recently on a radio show that statistics have shown that the black professional woman is making more inroads into the corporate world than black men. The dating and marriage prospects of professional, high-income black females are, for the most part, white men rather than black men. This results in more white/black relationships than in the past, according to the public radio broadcast. In this call-in show, they went on to say that one of the oldest stigmas attached to interracial relationships is that white men will sleep with black women but most likely will not marry them. One of the callers assumed that black men pursue white women more for status. The conversation was interesting but a bit narrow minded. I believe that we approach the subject of inter-racial marriage more open-mindedly today compared to twenty or thirty years ago. The best that any of us can do is to remain positive while holding our ground in regard to fundamental rights and protecting the dignity of each human being.

Not all interracial relationships are doomed. My family is living proof of that. My younger sister, Kiersten, has celebrated her twentieth year in a biracial marriage. That is not to say that they haven't had their share of challenges like most marriages, but they are raising three children who are being offered all the advantages of an upper middle class, two-parent family. My sister's husband is a terrific all-American guy, brought up in a Christian home. He is confident enough to have the courage of his convictions with no reservations. To him, love is love. With an open mind, love can also be colorblind.

After they were married, Ross' job transferred them to Memphis. Kiersten gave up her job as a result, but found another one in Memphis. Kiersten gave up working for several years when the kids were very young, but eventually resumed her career.

Their first child was Cole, now 18, who plays baseball like his dad, but also basketball. Chandler, a fifteen-year old young lady, was born two years after Cole, and has played a lot of tennis, starting when she was eight or nine years old. At this time in her life, however, she is turning from tennis to devoting more of her time to "girly-girl" activities with her friends, which doesn't please her mother. Kiersten would like for Chandler to go as far as possible in developing and improving her tennis game, rather than going along with her friends who prefer volleyball and soccer. Because her kids are given more, she expects them to take advantage of privileges, such as private lessons, that were never available as she was growing up. Her youngest, Schylar, who was eleven in November 2010, has a passion for soccer. Ross and Kiersten have exposed their children to opportunities in most sports, but are smart enough to know they can't push a sport down a child's throat.

L to R Front Row: Cole and Schylar - Back Row:
Chandler, Kiersten, and Ross

My sister, Valerie, is older than Kiersten. For most of her adult life, Valerie has wanted to be married, have children and enjoy Kiersten's lifestyle. Kiersten's life has contrasted starkly with Valerie's in the romance department. Valerie spent sixteen years in a love/hate relationship that never resulted in marriage. We all know, however, that no one's life is perfect, or even close. We found out something from Kiersten, however, that shocked all of us, but especially Valerie.

Kiersten was featured in a segment of an Oprah Winfrey show a few years back that dealt with privileged housewives who seemingly had it all: great husband, great house, great children, great job. When Oprah asked Kiersten if she was happy, she replied: "Miserable!"

Even though she is close to me as a sister, I cannot figure out why Kiersten is miserable. She has a successful career, plays in a tennis club (which she still loves), and seems to have many friends. Her kids attend private schools, and they have a beautiful home with all the outward trappings of success. I guess we will leave the fact that she is miserable for her and Ross to figure out. Their two girls and one boy have very light skin and look white, but my sister has been consistent in reminding them to never lose sight of the fact that in the eyes of society they are black or bi-racial. She has taught them to be proud of their black heritage and to respect Ross' white heritage as well, enjoying the best that both worlds have to offer. Kiertsen has recently joined an elite black social networking group so that her children can witness successful blacks in the corporate world to offset the negative image of black gangs, rappers and drug pushers.

We can more easily understand Valerie's situation and her perplexity than we can understand Kiersten's misery. Valerie's long relationship with a white man did not meet her expectations. He would not marry her, and she wanted to be his wife. Their breakup was not only racially motivated but also based on dishonesty, infidelity and mistrust. In short, they had different values and expectations. She also possesses our family's competitive nature, and that may be why she lasted sixteen years before giving up on the relationship.

Valerie, who has always envied Kiersten's married life, had her eyes opened when she heard about the remark made on the Oprah show. Valerie, probably the most creative of our family, re-invented herself after leaving the 16-year relationship with Dick in 1996. She made some drastic changes. Most people, when they go through changes may change hair styles, wardrobe, and make-up, that sort of thing. But Valerie took it to a different level when she legally changed her name. She is now Jaiden. She was given the opportunity to transfer within her Dublin-based company and chose a California location. She sold her condo in Columbus, and her company assumed expenses for her move. Although we were sorry to see her move so far away, we were proud of her gumption and independent spirit.

The new name definitely suits her personality! However, Mom and I haven't caught up with the new Valerie, and we have a problem calling her Jaiden. She, like Kiersten, is upbeat, outgoing, vibrant, and has a positive outlook and approach to life.

She supported herself well until the economic downsizing occurred in 2009. Jaiden, like so many others, did a 360-degree turn vocationally. When her IT job was eliminated, she relocated from California to Arizona, took a rigorous real estate course, and got her real estate license. She is doing well selling resort timeshares. Because she learned as a young tennis player that recovery after every shot is vital, she conducts her life in that manner. No matter how successful you become, a new shot may come your way. When that happens, you must prepare yourself to win the point. Even when you think you have won the point, you must be ready to recover in case the ball comes right back to you.

That difficult summer after Mark died became even darker. I was sued for "over defending" myself in the fight with the Muslim pro who resented my decision to put a woman in a place of authority over him. During the scuffle with him, I sustained an injury which made it difficult for me to walk, let alone play tennis! I thought my tennis career was over. My health insurance money was running out and I could barely teach. I had no funds left for a therapist, so I had to do my own version of physical therapy at a pool. I owe a debt of gratitude to Jim Criswell, Manager at Olympic, who supported me throughout this dark period. Fran McCabe, the desk clerk at Olympic, kept me mindful of walking with correct posture by daily reminders which were important to my successful rehabilitation.

One day, during physical therapy in the pool to strengthen my injured leg muscles, I walked off into the deep end. Since I couldn't use my injured leg to swim and any effort to get to the surface was unsuccessful, I slipped deeper under the water. Between the desperate push from my good leg and the strength in my arms, I managed to dog paddle to the surface and then to the edge of the pool. Part of me was disappointed that I'd made it.

In my frantic focus on trying to get well and constant worry about paying the bills, I had forgotten how to live a complete life. I was so consumed with the externals in my life, that I had lost touch with my essence. The near-drowning incident suddenly put my life in focus. As I began to relax about my recovery and work goals, I gradually put zest back into my life. In tennis we realize that the correct toss is an unconditional aspect of a good serve. It is foolish to focus on the serve without first looking at the toss. Likewise, before changing any one thing in life, we have to look at the most basic element involved in change.

We see the example of Jaiden, changing first her stifling relationship with a guy who wasn't equally devoted. Getting out of that relationship was the basic element for her change, and she built a new model of her life after making the most basic change. When examining the elements that comprised happiness for me at that time, I looked at the most essential element: my state of mind. When I took care of the anxieties that were blocking a peaceful state of mind, I knew what to do. I had to change myself from the inside out, not the other way. The external changes came when I was able to focus on the internal ones. "Changing the toss" in tennis is the first step to improving your serve. A good serve can win points. It took an incident where I could have died to make me look at basic changes I needed to make and to change my outlook on life.

I needed to get my social life, as well as my tennis career, back on track. Looking back, I think I may have been fighting depression over the pending lawsuit and my brother's death. The lawsuit was over at the end of summer with all eight jurors voting in my favor. It was an enormous weight lifted off my chest. My injury healed, and my life returned to normal.

In the spring of 1993, I heard about a few head tennis pro jobs opening up at local tennis clubs for the summer. Since being a head pro was one of my goals, and because head pros make more money, I interviewed for head pro jobs. I was turned down for all of them because the interviewers said I did not have country-club experience. The fact is that they hired less-qualified people for these positions. Instead of tennis pros, they hired school teachers for these jobs. I suspected I was being seen as a black man rather than a competent tennis pro. Black leaders such as Martin Luther King and Rosa Parks opened up many doors for me; but, not all doors had been opened. I was trying to break into a profession that was dominated by white males; and it was glaringly obvious, even to me, that I was black.

However, nothing stays the same. In 1995, I was fortunate to become the first black pro hired at Swim and Racquet Club. I made a little black history myself! I was not the head pro, but it was a big step toward that goal. I spent four enjoyable summers there, and the experience helped me make some notable inroads into the Columbus tennis circle beyond the Olympic Indoor Tennis Club.

Some notable black players were bringing positive attention to tennis. James Blake, a mixed race kid known for his speed and power, reached the finals in 2002 at the U.S. Open losing only to Andy Roddick. Blake played tennis in an Ivy League school before becoming professional and has a good solid game. However, he over hits and seems not always to have a game plan. He may need to work the points longer to stay in high ranks. Andy Roddick, an American favorite, comes off as one of the most talented players ever. However, he seems to come close very often but fails to grab the big trophies despite his huge amount of talent. He doesn't hit through the ball on his forehand as one would expect from someone of his size.

The well-known Williams' sisters, Venus and Serena, definitely give hope to thousands upon thousands of black kids around the country and around the world. Their strength is in their strength. Because of their powerful play, they "upped the ante" of Mary Carillo's Big Babe Tennis and set a target for others to reach. Well-known contemporaries of theirs – Kim Clijsters, Maria Sharapova and Justine Henin – are other high-achieving women in this sorority of powerful women tennis players who have set a new standard of excellence. I met the father of Venus and Serena once at the U.S. Open and we had a brief conversation. We agreed that Serena, a year or so younger than Venus, may be the better player.

Mr. Williams had a concept of what makes a great tennis player and paid attention to his own agenda. For instance, he had the girls skip playing as juniors and advance straight to the pro level. Ordinarily, that is not a wise strategy and can be self-destructive, but in their case it definitely worked. It worked because of the athletic abilities of the two women. Serena can be "high octane" at times, and her mouth can cost her money. Like other notable tennis players, she has at times berated line judges and umpires, incurring penalties as a result. Why does she do this? It may be a combination of intensity and will, but only she knows what compels her to do this in the heat of the moment as McEnroe and Connors did before her.

I continued to interview for head pro jobs, but was never hired. I think that part of the problem may have stemmed from my earlier trial and the wash-over from the world-renown trial of a famous football player, O. J. Simpson, who was found "not guilty." Blacks were cheering in clubs, and whites were both angry and disgusted. I felt that the verdict from this trial resulted in a setback of at least ten years for racial relations. The "trial of the century" made it even more difficult for black men like me to the extent that I entertained the idea of becoming a police officer and studied for a year to take the test. However, in the end I could not pass it. I have battled attention deficit disorder (ADD) my entire life and have suffered from "test taking anxiety." Knowing this, I knew my career would have to be something that would keep me moving and my mind active.

Mission accomplished! In the spring of 1999, I was finally hired as the head tennis pro at Medallion Country Club! It seems as if it took a long time to get what I worked for and wanted. I thought about Tiger Woods, the Williams sisters, and James Blake who had opened the country club doors to blacks. The first two years at Medallion were really satisfying. I had built several competitive tennis teams at Medallion, and many of the members followed me to Olympic for clinics in the winter. This provided much-improved income for me as well as many great friendships. By the third year we had three ladies' teams at Medallion. Everyone was working well together.

At that time in the world of tennis outside Columbus, Rafael Nadal, a phenomenal tennis player from Spain, was making his mark in the tennis world. I admired him instantly as a power-spin hitter whose technique seems unique to him. He has relentless power and spin on his forehand and a great slice on his backhand. He is so steady and fast that his defense turns into offense in the blink of an eye. Moving with phenomenal speed, he has a different way of hitting, or muscling, the ball. Not smooth like Roger Federer or Arthur Ashe, but moving like a jaguar, he brings excitement to the game.

Roger Federer emerged on the scene from Switzerland near the end of the twentieth century. He will go down as one of the very best tennis players in history. He reminds me of my idol, Arthur Ashe, because they both adopted one-handed backhands and were aggressive at the net. Ashe may have gone to the net more often than Federer, but their smoothness and shot-making are so splendid. Their strokes are so smooth that they remind me of a waterfall. Water flowing off a cliff, so natural, effortless, and graceful, comes to mind. They are also similar in composure because they do not let things get to them. They can "shake it off" and move on, letting their racquets do the talking. Even though there is a difference in their size, Ashe and Federer are more alike than different. Federer plays a mixture of old tennis (taking the net more like Ashe) but also adjusts to today's baseline players who stay back more. Federer's serve, too, is fluid like Ashe's.

My form was back in place as I was concentrating on first things first. This tremendous step inside the door of a white tennis club in Westerville reaffirmed my trust in people to make hiring decisions based on merit and not the outside appearance of the job candidate. My toss was high and I had delivered on my goal of a winning shot.

CHAPTER TEN

Tennis Tip: Don't run out of real estate.
When you go for shots, cross court or down the line, give
yourself enough room so you don't make errors. Sometimes
in doubles, I tell players to aim for the singles lines to give
themselves plenty of room to not err.

The winter of 2003 was a magical time in my life. I ran into an old girlfriend from college – Elise! I knew she was married and had children, but I didn't know she lived in Columbus. I was teaching a student whose mother knew Elise, and she mentioned to Elise that I was working at Olympic. Elise came and visited me there one day. We had a great conversation, spoke randomly and tried to stay in touch after her visit. Seeing her brought back a lot of old feelings. Even though she was married, I realized I still cared for her.

The indoor season passed and my business had gone well at Olympic, but I was dreading going back to Medallion Country Club. I liked the people, but the management was troubling. They called me in for a meeting to discuss all the progress that I had made during the previous summer. I thought I was in a position for a raise, but that bubble soon burst! When I entered the manager's office, he let me know that they had decided to reduce my salary significantly. They planned to take a good chunk of my salary to help pay for additional pros, he explained. That did not make sense to me.

Thad went on to explain: "You should be happy just to be in this county club setting." His saying that made less sense than his earlier statements. It was true that I had been happy, even thrilled, to be the head pro at that upscale club, but it appeared condescending for him to think that my gratefulness to be among the folks at Medallion superseded my need to make a salary in line with the responsibilities of the position. I was shocked, disappointed, and felt betrayed because I had grown the programs and had run the clinics and teams to perfection. The club was making money from its members, and I was attracting new members each summer. Some of the tennis players, when they found out about my raw deal, complained vociferously, and put some heat on the management about it. When that happened, Thad even threatened to get physical with me.

In my initial anger and disappointment, I told Thad that I would not return for the summer, but I thought longer about it and changed my mind. I hated to leave the people at Medallion who had signed up to be in my clinics. I negotiated a new contract with less of a salary cut and returned for the summer, but it would be my last summer there.

When I started back at Olympic Tennis in the fall, Elise called me and said she needed to talk to a friend. Tearfully, she told me her husband was having an affair and she did not know what to do. She was hurt, confused, furious, and numb. As the weeks passed, we talked less about her husband and more about the growing relationship between the two of us. One day Elise announced she was going to divorce her husband. That was the first time I felt free to hope that we could have a life together again after 25 years.

In the summer of 2004, Elise and I started dating again. Her divorce was not final, but she was ready to move on – with me. I was fully accepted by Elise's parents this time around. They thought I looked great compared to her (soon-to-be) ex-husband even though he is of their race! My race did not seem to matter anymore.

A new head pro job at Tartan Fields Golf and Tennis Club was offered to me and things were going well after the Medallion disaster. Tartan Fields presented a great opportunity for a new start and a chance to build another tennis program. The first year I was there, I had three ladies' teams, but they were not very competitive. My office was a golf cart because the club had not finished the clubhouse yet. By the third year, I had five ladies' teams and several juniors' clinics. Three of these ladies' teams went to the city championship. I was proud of the programs I had built at Tartan, and I enjoyed the people and the management. I thought I was going to retire at Tartan. However, once again my luck changed when the owners made some bad business decisions. My job at Tartan had gone well for three years, but the fourth year was a disaster because another tennis club, less than a mile away, had been built by the same owner. This split my teams, and the program fell apart. One of the two clubs dissolved as well. Just as in tennis, you can "run out of real estate" in life.

My tennis career always had its ups and downs. Luckily, my relationship with Elise had been good through those times of uncertainty. I was able to watch her children grow up. As great as that was, it was also hard watching Elise as a mom. I could not help but think about what it would have been like to have married Elise and to have had children with her.

The tennis precept at the start of this chapter reminds us of the need for caution in order to keep your tennis shot inside the court so that you don't run out of real estate. If you are playing doubles, a good method is to imagine that you have to stay inside the singles lines. That gives you a margin for error. So many times in life, we do not leave a margin for error, and that can result in lost opportunities. However, as hard as you may try to control the shots; when you play "doubles" in tennis, the success of your game is not solely under your control. You can play your best, and your partner can make enough errors that you lose the game. What can you do? Shake hands with your partner and opponents, say "good game" and proceed to the next challenge. In life, if you run out of real estate, look elsewhere and expand your opportunities by creating safe, yet winning, shots. Regrets are good only if you can learn and grow from bad shots or mistakes. Looking at bad decisions as feedback will shed a positive light on your game.

Late in the spring of 2008, I found out that Tartan would not need me for the summer. Summer job hunting had begun anew. When an opening was available at Worthington Hills Country Club, I took it even though it was not the head pro job. At least it was a job! I received a small salary and was able to teach lessons and provide clinics. The head pro, Amos Allison, was a former student and assistant of mine which bruised my ego a bit. However, I made the best of it with the help of Amos, who gave me a job there when I had few choices. I planned on returning the following summer because I really enjoyed the people and had a positive experience with the entire staff.

One of those special people was Denise Green, whom I had met along with her husband, Jim. Being lifelong tennis players, they enrolled in separate clinics with me. Jim is one of those natural athletic types, lean and well coordinated. He moves well on the court and has a winning attitude. Denise is always looking for improvement in her game. She hates to lose twice as much as she loves to win. Denise shared with me some thoughts about race and about life in general. I discovered a similarity between Denise's experiences and my own.

Denise moved into an all-white neighborhood when she was in middle school. Being very light skinned, she fit in well at first and enjoyed playing with the white kids on the street. Her happiness and peace of mind in her new neighborhood came to an abrupt halt the night her house was covered by smashed tomatoes. When she asked why this happened, her mother explained to her that word had gotten out that Denise's family was black, and white families feared that their property values were going to plunge as a result of having a black family on the block.

She learned later that additional prejudice, born of hatred and fear, had been the catalyst for the tomato-bashing of their house. It appeared to neighbors that Denise's mother was white, because she was so light-skinned that she could pass for white, but Denise's step-father was black because he was very dark-skinned. Up until then, the fact that Denise's mother was fair-skinned had been a "plus" as it had been for my mom. Being able to "pass" for white had helped her get good jobs and move her family into a predominately white neighborhood. Now, her fair skin was working against her because of the perception of the white neighbors.

The neighbors believed that a black man and a white woman lived among them. For blacks, moving into a white neighborhood was risky enough in the 1960s, but an "interracial" couple was far worse. In that time period and in that neighborhood, such intermingling was totally unacceptable. "The prejudice was mostly economic" claims Denise. But, economic or otherwise, after that incident Denise quit going out into the street to play. Instead, she stayed inside and watched from the window as others played her favorite games like jump rope and hide-and-seek.

Denise, a Catholic, attended parochial schools for all but the sixth-grade. She attended six different schools in as many years. In sixth grade she attended a public school in Cleveland. "That year of public school set me back a whole year in instruction. When I returned to my Catholic school, I was stressed to keep up even though I had been an excellent student when I left fifth grade."

Prejudice in the parochial schools was minimal and divided equally among all those who were different from the mainstream population. "A Chinese girl was picked on as were other minority kids such as Polish and Italian kids." Overall, Denise felt accepted among her schoolmates from grades one through twelve. Her high school was not only a Catholic school, but also an all-girl school. This limited her "real-world" exposure and considerably narrowed or eliminated potential problems of racial intermingling and dating in high school. Her social life consisted of singing in a choir and doing things as a group with the other students. It was not until college that she began dating, and then not much, because she was rather shy and academically, more than socially, oriented.

Beating down another stereotype concerning black families in America is this couple's difference in religion.

Popular culture assigns blacks to southern Baptist or "holy-roller" churches, prone to "shouting, swooning and fainting as they get the spirit." Denise's husband, Jim, is Baptist. No matter how much she tries, Denise remains uncomfortable in black churches. Having been steeped in the formal liturgy and predictable order of worship of the Catholic church, she has trouble accommodating to the emotional and noisy worship in black churches and continues to feel strange in Jim's church. Even though Denise is musically gifted, the music she sang in church choirs was classical, rather than gospel, which adds to the difference in worship style between her and Jim.

Denise's discomfort in the black church reminds me of my roommate, Joe, who was more comfortable with blacks than I was, despite our color difference. Her experience in the black church brings home the fact that race does not determine feelings of comfort or discomfort. The supposition that blacks are protestant may be another stereotype or subtle form of prejudice. Joe, being white, was more comfortable in the ghetto because he had been raised there among blacks and had been imprinted accordingly. He was more "black" in the ghetto than I. Accordingly, it is safe to assume that a white southern Baptist would be more comfortable than Denise in a black church due to conditioning or imprinting experiences there.

In college as in high school, most of Denise's friends continued to be white. She, like I, had been imprinted by her environment in that regard. She had trouble relating to blacks because of the unfamiliarity they presented. For instance, she never had a black roommate and her choice of music was not black. Instead of Aretha Franklin, Denise preferred the group: Peter, Paul and Mary. Rather than consciously seeking out one side or the other – black or white – she thinks her conservative Catholic upbringing and neighborhood determined her choices.

Denise met her husband of 30 years at Ohio State. Jim is black with a darker color and perhaps a stronger racial identify. Denise says that she doesn't think of herself as a black woman particularly. When she sees a black family in her affluent, white neighborhood, she states: "I notice that they are different and stand out." However, she doesn't apply the same degree of "difference" to herself. Denise has one particular woman friend who is black. She met this friend when she and Jim played tennis with the other couple. The two couples have remained close beyond two decades. Most of her friends, though, are white.

She has felt the sting of prejudice from blacks more than whites. Blacks singled her out because of her light skin color. Throughout childhood and adolescence, the name she was called was "high yellow." This refers to her light skin and reaches back to slavery. Lighter-skinned blacks were preferred by slave masters and given a higher status.

Some blacks believe that "high yellow" custom still prevails. For instance, the entry of blacks into management or executive positions in business is perceived to be easier if they are of a lighter skin color. This kind of belief dies hard because it has lingered so long. Because one's color is completely beyond one's control, it hurts when people use it to explain one's accomplishment.

Denise's face turns sad when she recalls "I have been told that my career advancement would not have occurred as quickly - or maybe not at all - if I had been a dark-skinned black woman."

Even though she has confidence in herself and her gifts, she realizes that the harsh perception some people use to explain, if not excuse, the advancement of blacks remains. "If you let it," she says, "it can make you furious. It can make less-secure people begin to doubt themselves; and, as a result, diminish their determination to succeed."

It matters very little whether "high yellow" is used by whites or blacks to diminish a person. The effect is the same. My mother mentioned the effect it had on her as she was growing up. She has lived with the advantages, but also the disadvantages, of being black with a light skin tone.

In a subsequent discussion over coffee at her kitchen table, Denise elaborated further on this evaluation of worth by skin tone as being a learned behavior. She thinks it begins as soon as a child enters the process of socialization. Her five-year-old granddaughter, Alexis, is already testing the waters when she asks Denise which doll (a light or dark skinned one) Denise prefers. In an attempt to deflect the question, Denise focuses on another aspect of the difference between the two dolls: the outfits the dolls wear. "I like the little yellow skirt or the blue top she is wearing." However, Lexie won't let her off the hook until Denise gives her a pat answer. "Which doll?" she continues to ask. Lexie prefers the white one. The question bothers Denise because of the implications about race and the fact that Lexie already feels that white is more desirable than black.

Jim tries, too, to offset traditional assumptions, such as the color of Santa Claus, by collecting black Santas. His collection focuses on black Santas in different vocations, such as a fireman Santa and a physician Santa. Jim's thinks that "children will pay attention to occupations, and race may become less of an issue." Denise hopes that their home, which is abundant with art and books from the African culture, will give the children more appreciation of their black heritage as they continue to grow and examine their fit in society.

Their grandson, Devin (age 10), brings color into question when they are walking on a warm summer morning. "Grandmother, you are white, but Lexie and I are black. Just look at our arms." Denise volleys that question by saying that they are three different shades on a continuum of white to black. "I am lighter than Devin, and Devin is lighter than Lexie." As they look at each other, she adds that "Our friend, Francie (who is white), may be a shade darker than Grandma, especially in the summertime." Denise is adroit in explaining that "different" does not mean better or worse, but admits that it is hard to combat outside influences that may have stronger weight as the kids become socialized by their peers and the wider society.

When they were younger and their two daughters were the ages of their grandchildren, Denise and Jim were victims of racial discrimination as they tried to buy a house in a white neighborhood. Their racial roadblock resulted in a lawsuit which they won. Going back farther on the same subject, Denise discusses renting an apartment when she was in college. She reminisces that when she and girlfriends looked for an apartment, she'd linger behind until the white girls secured the place rather than complicate or endanger the rental. "You have to work the system."

Even today, shopping at high-end stores calls for a consciousness concerning how she dresses, a conscious decision to avoid prejudice, one that white women do not have to deal with. She went on to explain how this works. Recently, when she dashed into a store early in the morning before she'd had a chance to apply makeup or dress in her usual well-coordinated manner, she saw a white colleague from afar and suffered a slight panic. She was highly intent on avoiding being seen by the other woman. Denise purposely chose the check-out counter located the farthest away from the woman, practically a football-field size away. She laughs as she tells me this. I don't. I suppose it could be humorous, but it is also sad.

Denise quickly admits that "being black, or biracial, in American society definitely takes more energy because you always have to be on guard." Stated or not, she says, there is always a conscious awareness of being accepted, always some overt effort to fit in. "Whether it is good, bad, or ugly, it has been imprinted on me to be accepted where I am. That takes work."

Denise's life has contained more success than failure in the area of real estate. The tennis connotation of "real estate" (and errors you can make when you run out of it or don't give yourself enough room) enters my mind when I wonder about "what-ifs" in my own life. About a year ago, I ran into Lana. She remarried after her divorce and has a beautiful daughter, Madison, whom she brought to Olympic for a tennis lesson. I now teach Madison twice a week. I reflect on "what could have been" with Lana and wonder if we would have had a daughter and if I would have been a good father.

The tennis precept at the start of this chapter cautions us to give ourselves enough room so that we don't make errors or run out of real estate. I remember that Lana and I had given ourselves room – time apart – during our relationship in order to prevent errors. Even that was not enough. The "real estate" she was after would have had a dentist's shingle attached. After seeing her daughter, I couldn't help telling Lana that we would have had cute kids.

CHAPTER 11

Tennis Tip: Don't celebrate your victory until the last shot is fired. The time most likely to lose a game is right after you have broken your opponent's serve because you may have a tendency to feel a false sense of security. It's important to play as hungry for the point when you are leading as you do when you are behind.

Several tennis students and friends that I have taught remind me of different perspectives on being black and dealing with a majority white race in America. I had a tennis student, Chris, who was biracial and was having a hard time at school. He said he felt like an outcast and was trying to find his identity. I took to him because I could relate to him and his feelings. Chris and I went to the movies and shared some great conversations about race. His mother was black and his father was white. He was living with his white grandparents. For the most part, his friends didn't see color, but the words of the few that did hurt. One time Chris said he felt all alone at his school. I told him that he will find more and more people who are "mentally color blind" like we are, and they will like him for who he is, not being influenced by the color of his skin. "These are the kids that will be your true and lasting friends."

A few of my other students have discussed with me experiences similar to, yet different from, those of Chris. Miles Harrris, a former Davis Cup student of mine, will start college in the fall of 2010. He interned with a tennis pro at a country club during the summer of 2010. Miles was graduated from a Catholic school in Columbus. In middle school he went to a public school where about 35% of the school was black. For the first time his best friends were black. "Some of them said that I acted different, not black, and I was called 'Oreo.'"

Miles feels comfortable around anyone – black or white - who accepts him for who he is. "There has never been a day in my life where I forget that I'm an African American. To forget my color would be like forgetting who I am."

Even though he has encountered racism from whites a few times in life, he no longer lets racism faze him. "I look at it as ignorance and think to myself that I'm more mature than to stoop that low."

Another friend, Kathy Starks, moved from a predominantly black neighborhood and school district to an upper middle class setting at the beginning of sixth grade. She found herself traumatized by the cultural shift. She changed from a former chatter-box to a student who never raised her hand in class and became extremely quiet and withdrawn. Kathy, a formerly successful student, had to take summer school in order to continue with her class to seventh grade after the first year in the new school.

Gradually, during high school, she made friends with both black and white girls in her new setting. Moreover, Kathy's neighborhood was a small black enclave in the suburban village. As soon as she got off the school bus and returned to the security of her block, she felt perfectly at home and at ease. She enjoyed a wonderful home life and many of the neighborhood women were like second moms to her.

Gradually Kathy was able to relax more with whites as she continued in the white-dominated culture; but her ease with blacks diminished. She was often accused of "talking white" or "acting white." When she attended events in an all-black setting, she was nervous because she had lost touch with the black culture in ways such as dance moves. The result was that she began to feel that she didn't really succeed socially with either black or white boys, so dating became a big hassle. As Kathy navigated through black and white social scenes, such as high school athletic events, she realized that she felt more comfortable in her white suburban setting than in her former neighborhood.

The black Baptist church served to keep Kathy grounded, but the white experience in high school acted as a catalyst for Kathy's college success. She felt comfortable with her white college roommates. The first year of college helped to synthesize the two cultures in which Kathy was living. The synthesis came about in this manner. A black male student was accused of raping a white student which caused a general state of rage among the college's black students. The student who was charged was a track star and half the size of the purported victim. Because he fit the general description the girl gave to police, the police went after him and only him. This race to convict based on shallow evidence caused black students to unite and engage in a "sit-in" in the office of the college president. Kathy joined the group of protesters. Eventually charges were dropped against the black student.

"The impact on me was profound," she claims, "for I found courage to stand up for my people." This life-changing event enabled her to step out of her shyness and become more confident in her abilities.

Kathy, now close to fifty years of age, has developed into a confident, self assured woman who approaches life with an optimistic attitude. When problems arise, such as being in an environment where people are cool to her, she thinks about race as the last reason for her discomfort. Because Kathy is well adjusted, she makes friends easily. She recently celebrated her fiftieth birthday in Boca Raton with six friends: three happen to be black; the other three happen to be white. She says, "I can't ask for better than that."

Dane Shavers, another of my students, grew up in northern Ohio, and had a situation similar to Kathy's. His family moved into a white suburban area with large houses and well-kept lawns when he was only ten months old. Only blacks lived on his particular street, but the housing development, as a whole, contained mostly whites. Dane shared that most of the problems were between blacks and Italians, but that dissipated after sixth grade and people got along.

Dane was the only black in his classes throughout high school. Therefore, dating was a problem. Because he and his black friends had all grown up together on that one particular block, a kind of oasis in that one small housing development, they knew each other very well; in fact, too well for dating. They felt as if they were one big family, and you don't date your sisters and brothers. Most of his girl friends were white, and that presented no problems in the 70's as he was coming of age. He thinks his success in dating white girls stemmed from the fact that he was a well-respected athlete. He dated cheerleaders and other white girls whose parents accepted him. Likewise, college dating of white girls was no problem for Dane. "Black guys didn't say much when they saw me with a white girl."

These young men - Chris, Miles, and Dane - know that they have to fit in, adjust to their surroundings and never become complacent about their chances for success. In many ways they realize they may have to work a little harder than their white friends in order to disprove misconceptions about their limitations. People, whether young people, or old, can still be victims of what they were "carefully taught" about other groups as they developed from child to adult. In talking with these young men, I found in their frank discussion, hope and promise about their future and a genuine gratitude to be where they are.

Kathy and Denise have reached middle age and seem content that they have attained their goals. I believe that they, as well as the three young men, have successfully navigated both worlds: the white and black worlds of their existence. They have capitalized on their strengths and ignored any weaknesses, especially weaknesses perceived by others.

The precept of "not celebrating the victory until the last shot is fired" reminds us that most blacks still see a need to stay on guard in order to be successful in America. An aura of caution surrounds them. They can never forget about race. They can never completely exhale, as Denise alludes to when she speaks of being dressed up and wearing make-up whenever she goes shopping even if it's early in the morning. However, if you look very carefully at most people, beyond race and ethnicity, you will find that they are doing the best they can with what they know. We must continue to teach each other.

AFTERWORD

The world has gotten smaller in the past fifty years, resulting in greater intermingling among the races. Ethnic diversity is commonly encountered as one looks, for example, at encampments along beaches, where families on a blanket may be comprised of two or three different colors. Accepting different races on your "beach blanket" or in your home is an outward sign of accord and comfort among diverse races.

That is not to say that prejudice no longer exists in America. For example, one can see friction between blacks and Somalis in our own city. Their common prejudice begins with lack of understanding about cultural differences which can result in fear. Struggling blacks may fear that their jobs may be endangered by these new immigrants, and housing conditions may crowd them and force them together physically before they are ready to get to know one another. Public schools have the responsibility of educating this new flock of American youth who may be entering school for the first time when they are 15 years of age or older. The population of some Columbus City Schools is more than 50% Somali and Hispanic. White students are a minority. Both a burden and an opportunity are presented as the American public accepts the children of Somali and other countries with diverse customs and values.

Even though he retired from tennis in 1980, my hero, Arthur Ashe, never left the public eye. On February 6, 1993, Mr. Ashe died from the disease of AIDS because of a blood transfusion that he had during heart surgery. Married and with a small child at the time, he bore the death sentence of AIDS with the same dignity and poise with which he had conducted his life up to that time. After he made the announcement about his disease to the public, a reporter asked him: "Mr. Ashe, I guess this must be the heaviest burden you have ever had to bear, isn't it?" After hesitating to think for a minute, he replied: "No, it isn't . . . Being black is the greatest burden I've had to bear."

The fall of 2008 brought America's racial attitudes to the forefront of most conversations in America. For the first time we had a biracial man running for president. Many people asked me how I felt about a black man being President of the United States. I answered that

I liked candidate Barack Obama for his policies and would vote for him. However, I would not vote for him simply because he was black. I knew, on the other hand, that my sister, Kiersten (as well as many other blacks), would vote for him for that reason alone. Kiersten, like many blacks, felt it was important to spread black pride across America, and that feeling trumped their objectivity about policies or politics.

Obama's election to the office of President demonstrated to me that America had come a long way in the struggle for racial equality. When I reflect on John Lewis, Dr. King, the Freedom Riders and other white, as well as black, men and women who struggled for Civil Rights in America, I recall once again the words of Dr. King that "The arc of the moral universe is long, but it bends toward justice." Things take time, and we need to have faith. Global intermingling keeps us aware that our fear of people that don't look like us must be replaced by trust in others and a willingness to improve health, education, and childcare for all people across cultures.

It still puzzles me, however, that a man who is biracial (half black and half white) is considered black and not white. Who made up that law? I guess the slave owners made up those "laws" to protect their holdings. Even an outwardly "white" person with an ounce of black blood is considered black. When light-skinned blacks were caught "passing" as whites in order to improve their economic lot and make a strike toward freedom, their punishment was severe. Other groups, such as Jews and Native Americans who have suffered severe discrimination have persevered and prospered in America but have had to work hard in order to do so.

It is time to take a different look at this. At the end of the first decade of the twenty-first century, isn't it time for biracial people to choose the race that they want to be identified with? That might help to simplify cultural questions and reduce conflicts. Perhaps the census needs to be modified to broaden categories.

Communication in a tennis (doubles) match is vitally important. Your partner can see what's behind you and out of your line of vision. Therefore, he can help you by calling for the shot – "Mine" – or yelling "Switch!" Switching means that you and your partner change sides until the point is over. It takes that kind of looking out for one another and communicating in order to win a doubles match. Communication among the races is vital in order for everyone to come out winners. The president, who is a talented communicator, sets a high standard for Americans to reason together and to problem-solve with one another. His greatest talent as a communicator may be that he can appear cool under pressure. He is calm and deliberate in his reactions and chooses his tone and words carefully in order to communicate effectively. Obama knows that both Democrats and Republicans need one another and need to communicate effectively in order for the country to thrive.

We don't have time to fight about color in our country any longer. There are people out there who don't care about our color. They just want to destroy our way of life. We didn't deserve what happened on"nine-eleven," but it did bring our nation together. We should not need a terrorist attack for this to happen. I know one thing for sure. When more people are infected with "mental color blindness", we will have fewer social problems. It is time to be one nation and focus on our national colors of red, white and blue.

Chris has become a good tennis player and I see him often at the courts. I hope to continue to be available to him and mentor him through his high school years. I want to convey to him, and anyone else who is biracial, what my parents taught me: that it is important for each person to look at himself as "unique" and that "different" does not mean better or worse. That, quite simply, is good advice for everyone. Currently, my personal life is going well. Elise and I are still dating and see each other as much as we can. I am proud of her for going back to college and achieving her goal of teaching elementary school full-time. It is curious that it took twenty-five years and a lot of twists and turns of life for us to get back together.

I am currently the Davis Cup Captain for the Ohio Valley. The Davis Cup is an international tennis competition where the highest ranking students in every country compete against similarly ranked opponents. For example, America's best competes against the best of Colombia. I coach children from ages 12-17 who are for the most part nationally ranked for Davis Cup. I use a quotation with my students from the revered tennis player, Arthur Ashe, who said: "A competitive athlete never gives up. He may run out of time, but he never gives up." He added, "Never betray an inward sense of defeat." That attitude helps make my students better players and, more importantly, better people.

I believe that we are imprinted by our early childhood environment, but we can choose our outlook and behavior as we interact with others. People change their attitudes and behaviors when they see a need to do so. As a student, and later a teacher of tennis, I have had the pleasure of seeing myself and others change as we learn to believe in ourselves and become successful in using talents that we may not have discovered had it not been for tennis.

My tennis career has provided me opportunities to work with adults, teenagers and children on a daily basis. As I witness growth in my students while they learn and become proficient at tennis, I continue to learn and understand myself. Their joy becomes mine. Someone once said that, when you enjoy your work, it is no longer work. A satisfying career, even with its ups and downs, contributes greatly to a meaningful life. It is fun to share my experiences with the kids. I can't imagine doing anything else in my life.

As I bring closure to this book, I would like to leave the reader with the thought that I have deliberated about my life and its relevance to the lives of others. I continue to be energized by the opportunity I have to make a difference as I work with students from 8 to 80. To observe improvement in skills and to see delight on their faces when they make a tennis shot that they thought was impossible, is highly gratifying. My students know that the game is hard, but hard work leads to success. The game of tennis requires effort and discipline which result in success, but a good instructor keeps it fun at the same time. Winning at tennis means that you give your best and then move on.

INDEX

Made in the USA
Charleston, SC
20 March 2011